THE UNIVERSITY
OF CHICAGO
CONSORTIUM ON CHICAGO
SCHOOL RESEARCH

RESEARCH REPORT   MARCH 2015

Discipline Practices in Chicago Schools
Trends in the Use of Suspensions and Arrests

W. David Stevens, Lauren Sartain, Elaine M. Allensworth, and Rachel Levenstein
with Shannon Guiltinan, Nick Mader, Michelle Hanh Huynh, and Shanette Porter

TABLE OF CONTENTS

1 Executive Summary

Introduction
5 Growing Concerns about the Use of Exclusionary Disciplinary Practices

Chapter 1
11 Trends in Exclusionary Discipline Practices in CPS

Chapter 2
21 Reasons for Suspensions and Police Involvement

Chapter 3
27 Perceptions of School Safety and Order

Chapter 4
31 Interpretive Summary

35 References

37 Appendices A-D

ACKNOWLEDGEMENTS

We are grateful to the Chicago Public Schools for providing us the administrative data that allowed us to do this work. Staff at CPS, especially Karen van Ausdal and Justina Schlund, were helpful in offering clarity around discipline policies in the district. We thank our Steering Committee members for their thoughtful comments, in particular Aarti Dhupelia, Chris Jones, and Lila Leff for reading the report thoroughly. This report benefited from feedback from our fellow researchers at the University of Chicago Consortium on Chicago School Research (UChicago CCSR), in particular Jennie Jiang and Stacy Ehrlich. UChicago CCSR communications team members, especially Bronwyn McDaniel and Jessica Puller, provided assistance in publishing this report. We are also thankful for CPS administrators who took their time to share their experiences with discipline in their school buildings. The Atlantic Philanthropies provided generous funding for this line of research, which made this report possible. Finally, we also gratefully acknowledge the Spencer Foundation and the Lewis-Sebring Family Foundation, whose operating grants support the work of UChicago CCSR.

This report was produced by UChicago CCSR's publications and communications staff: Emily Krone, Director for Outreach and Communication; Bronwyn McDaniel, Senior Manager for Outreach and Communication; and Jessica Puller, Communications Specialist.

Graphic Design: Jeff Hall Design
Photography: Cynthia Howe, David Schalliol
Editing: Ann Lindner

03.2015/pdf/jh.design@rcn.com

Executive Summary

The Chicago Public Schools (CPS) have initiated a number of reforms to reduce the use of exclusionary practices that remove students from the classroom, like suspensions. This report, the first in a series on discipline practices in CPS, provides an overview of the use of suspensions and arrests in Chicago schools and the degree to which practices have changed from 2008-09 to 2013-14.

Districts and policymakers across the United States are in the midst of a fundamental shift in how they approach school discipline. During the 1980s and 1990s, schools increasingly enacted discipline policies that mandated the use of suspensions, expulsions, and police arrests for student misconduct. In recent years, the general public, policymakers, and school administrators, from the federal level down, have strongly questioned this approach. Critics highlight the growing number of schools with very high suspension rates, as well as inequities in suspension rates by race, gender, family income, special education status, and sexual orientation.[1] They point out that students who are suspended or expelled are more likely to struggle academically and drop out of school.[2] There is evidence that students who attend schools with zero-tolerance approaches to discipline are also likely to experience negative school environments.[3] As a result, national and local policymakers have called on schools to reduce the use of exclusionary disciplinary practices—those that remove students from the classroom (see box *Definitions of Key Terms* on p.8 for a description of various discipline practices we highlight in this report).

Key Findings

Out-of-school suspensions have been declining in CPS, but are still given frequently, especially at the high school level. In 2013-14, about 1-in-7 high school students (16 percent) received an out-of-school suspension (OSS). This number is down from the highest point in the 2009-10 school year when about 1-in-4 high school students (24 percent) received an OSS. Since 2009-10, OSS rates in high schools have declined each year. At the middle grades level (grades 6-8), OSS rates were unchanged, at around 13-14 percent from 2008-09 to 2012-13, but they dropped in the 2013-14 school year to 10 percent.

The average length of suspensions has also been declining over time, with the largest drop occurring in the 2012-13 school year. This drop coincided with changes to the CPS Student Code of Conduct (SCC) which explicitly constrained the use of long suspensions.

The decline in high school OSS rates has been accompanied by a doubling of in-school suspension rates among African American high school students. In the 2013-14 school year, 15 percent of high school students received at least one in-school suspension

---

1 Dawson (1991); Fabelo, Thompson, Plotkin, Carmichael, Marchbanks, & Booth (2011); Himmelstein & Brückner (2010); Osher, Bear, Sprague, & Doyle (2010).
2 Balfanz, Byrnes, & Fox (2013); Fabelo et al. (2011).
3 Schreck & Miller (2003); Steinberg, Allensworth, & Johnson (2011).

(ISS). In-school suspensions are given more frequently to African American students than students of other racial/ethnic groups and the use of in-school suspensions have been increasing over time. ISS rates nearly doubled for African American high schools students between 2008-09 and 2013-14, but remained the same for other student groups. In-school suspensions are rare outside of the high schools; 4 percent of middle grades students received an ISS in the 2013-14 school year.

Some schools may be using in-school suspensions in instances where they previously used out-of-school suspensions, or shortening the length of out-of-school suspensions while also giving students a day or two of ISS. In-school suspensions tend to be shorter than out-of-school suspensions and they allow for the possibility that students could receive an intervention or support while serving the suspension. Yet, they still result in a loss of instructional time for students.

Suspension rates are strongly related to students' prior test scores, their race, and their gender. African American students are much more likely to be suspended than students of other races/ethnicities. Suspension rates are particularly high for African American boys in high school. About a third of African American boys in high school (33 percent) received an OSS in 2013-14. In comparison, 13 percent of Latino boys in high school and 6 percent of white/Asian high school boys received an OSS in 2013-14. African American girls also have high OSS rates in high school, at 23 percent in 2013-14. This compares to high school OSS rates of 6 percent for Latina girls and 2 percent for white/Asian girls. ISS rates are also much higher for African American students than for Latino or white/Asian students.

Suspension rates are also high for students with disabilities and for students who begin the school year with test scores that are below average. OSS rates for students with identified disabilities were 24 percent at the high school level and 16 percent in middle grades in the 2013-14 school year. Among students with low test scores (scores in the bottom quartile in the prior school year), suspension rates are also very high: 27 percent received an OSS at the high school level and 17 percent received an OSS at the middle school level in the 2013-14 year. Thus, students who start the year with the weakest academic skills are more likely than other students to receive a suspension that removes them from classroom instruction.

Most suspensions in high schools result from acts of student defiance—where students refuse to comply with adults' demands. At the high school level, about 60 percent of out-of-school suspensions and almost all in-school suspensions result from defiance of school staff, disruptive behaviors, and school rule violations. While administrators we interviewed recognized fights as a primary concern in their schools, 27 percent of out-of-school and 7 percent of in-school suspensions in high school are for physical conflict or threats to safety, meaning most suspensions result from conflicts that involve no physical harm. In the middle grades, conflicts between students and acts of defiance toward teachers account for most out-of-school suspensions, at about equal rates.

Arrests for incidents at school are uncommon, though African American high school boys are more likely to be arrested than other students. In the 2011-12 school year (the most recent year for which we have Chicago Police Department data), 1.8 percent of high school students and 1.1 percent of middle grades students were arrested for incidents occurring at school. Arrest rates were twice as high among African American boys as for the district as a whole—3.6 percent of African American high school boys enrolled in CPS were arrested for at-school incidents in the 2011-12 school year, which is about 1-in-28 students. In comparison, 1.6 percent of Latino boys and 2 percent of African American girls and fewer than 1 percent of white/Asian students or Latina girls in high school were arrested for at-school events.

Students are arrested more often for incidents that occur outside of school than for incidents at school. Over 4 percent of CPS high school students were arrested in the 2011-12 school year for incidents occurring outside of school. Combining arrests inside of school and outside of school, 6 percent of CPS students were arrested in the 2011-12 school year.

Schools tend only to involve police in incidents for which the SCC requires police notification. Incidents for which police notification is optional but not required solicit police notification only 22 percent of the time. Even when an infraction is serious enough to *require* police notification, schools only notify police 43 percent of the time.

When they occur, infractions that involve drugs or weapons are most likely to result in a police notification. That is, about one out of every three incidents that involve drugs or weapons at a school result in police involvement. However, drug and weapons infractions represent a small portion of the discipline infractions at schools, so they are not the source of most arrests. Physical altercations, or physical fights among students, are the source of most police involvement at schools.

Arrest rates for both in-school and out-of-school incidents have declined over time for CPS students. The declines in arrest rates have been driven by declining arrest rates for African American boys, who have consistently been much more likely to be arrested than other students. Both out-of-school arrests and in-school arrests of CPS students declined after 2009-10, up until 2011-12.

At the same time that OSS rates and arrests have declined, students and teachers are reporting that they feel safer at school. At the high school level, student perceptions of safety and teacher perceptions of order have been improving since the 2008-09 school year; this is also the period during which OSS rates declined in high schools. At the middle grades level, there have been only marginal improvements in students' feelings of safety at school. However, there was a more marked improvement in the 2013-14 school year, which was the first year that OSS rates declined in the middle grades.

This research suggests three major areas of focus if the district is to reduce the use of exclusionary disciplinary practices in Chicago schools:

1. **High schools.** Students are suspended at all grade levels, but very high suspension rates in high schools account for 56 percent of out-of-school suspensions districtwide. If the district is to reduce the use of suspensions and disciplinary disparities substantially, it will require changes in high school practices. Efforts aimed at lower grades will do little to reduce the overall use of exclusionary practices in CPS, unless there are concurrent changes in high schools.

2. **Disparities in suspensions for African American students, especially for African American boys, and for students with low incoming achievement.** While students of all races are occasionally suspended, suspension rates are much higher for African American students, and especially high for boys. Students with low incoming test scores are also at high risk for being suspended.

   The fact that high suspension rates persist for certain groups of students, despite policy efforts aimed at reducing the use of exclusionary practices, suggests a need for better support around reducing exclusionary practices in schools and classrooms that serve student groups with a higher likelihood of being suspended.

3. **Prevention and de-escalation of conflict, especially between students and teachers.** Most suspensions and arrests at school are a result of conflict between students and teachers—such as disobedience and defiance—or conflicts among students, especially in high schools. This suggests a need for increased training for teachers and school staff to prevent and de-escalate conflict, as well as to develop students' social-emotional skills, particularly at schools with high suspension rates.

This is the first in a series of reports on discipline practices in CPS. The next report will show how the use of exclusionary and non-exclusionary practices varies considerably across schools in the district and describe the types of schools that rely on particular practices. It will also describe the ways in which the disciplinary practices of the school are related to the quality of the school climate and the instructional environments in classrooms. The third report will examine the use of alternative and preventative discipline strategies in CPS schools. Other research will evaluate the consequences of changes in disciplinary policies for changes in school practices around discipline as well as changes in school climate and instruction.

INTRODUCTION

Growing Concerns about the Use of Exclusionary Disciplinary Practices

Districts and policymakers across the United States are in the midst of a fundamental shift in how they approach school discipline.

By the late 1990s, most school districts across the country had instituted "zero-tolerance" discipline policies for incidents involving violence, weapons, drugs, or alcohol.[4] These policies mandated automatic use of school suspensions, expulsions, and police arrests, with minimal allowances for individual circumstances to be taken into account.[5] In some schools, even relatively minor infractions were uniformly addressed with suspension from class. The theory was that tough uniform enforcement of policies for all offences would prevent more serious offences from occurring. However, over the past few years, there has been growing concern about the use of exclusionary disciplinary practices—those that remove students from the school or classroom, such as suspensions and arrests in schools. As a result, there is now a movement to reduce the use of these exclusionary disciplinary practices.

One of the concerns about exclusionary disciplinary practices is that they are over-used. Across the country, over two million middle and high school students are suspended at least once during the school year. Nationally, suspension rates for high school students increased from 8 percent in 1975 to 11 percent in 2010.

That means that more than 1-in-10 high school students were suspended in 2010 across the country. Over 2,600 secondary schools suspend 25 percent or more of their total student enrollment.[6] One study found that 54 percent of all Texas students were assigned an in-school suspension (ISS) and 33 percent were assigned an out-of-school suspension (OSS) at least once between seventh and twelfth grade.[7]

Another concern about the use of exclusionary disciplinary practices is that they may be administered unfairly, based on students' backgrounds. There are significant disparities in suspension rates across student groups. Nationally, suspension rates for African American middle and high school students are 17 percentage points higher than for white students.[8] In Illinois, there is a 21 percentage point gap between the rates of exclusionary practices for African American and white students in K-12 settings.[9] Male African American high school students are especially vulnerable to being suspended compared to other groups: nationally they are suspended at rates 20 percentage points higher than white males.[10] Students with disabilities are twice as likely to be suspended as other

---

4 Heaviside, Rowand, Williams, & Farris (1998).
5 Shah & McNeil (2013).
6 Losen & Martinez (2013).
7 Fabelo et al. (2011).
8 Losen, Hewitt, & Toldson (2014).
9 Losen & Gillespie (2012).
10 Losen & Martinez (2013).

students and LGBT youth are at greater risk than heterosexual peers.[11] Yet some research suggests there may be few differences in the quantity or quality of misbehavior between students of different racial, ethnic, and status groups.[12]

A final concern is that exclusionary practices are ineffective for improving student behavior and school climate and may even lead to worse outcomes for students and a more problematic school environment for learning. These concerns are based on research showing that suspensions and expulsions are strongly associated with negative outcomes for students and for schools. For example, students who are expelled or suspended are more likely to fail courses, repeat grades, and drop out of school than other students.[13] Prior research from the University of Chicago Consortium on Chicago School Research (UChicago CCSR) showed that schools that give out more suspensions have lower levels of safety—even among schools serving similar populations of students who are from similar neighborhoods.[14] One study found that African American students were more likely to experience racism and unfairness in schools with higher rates of detention and suspension.[15] Policy statements from the American Academy of Pediatrics, and the American Psychological Association have come out strongly against zero-tolerance discipline policies and the over-use of suspensions, noting negative educational, social, and health consequences that often result from the punishments themselves.[16]

In response to these concerns, states and school districts across the country are now attempting to reduce their use of exclusionary discipline practices.[17] The U.S. Department of Justice and the Department of Education have been encouraging schools to reduce the rates at which they use exclusionary practices for student misbehavior since 2009. In January 2014, they issued strong guidelines intended to reduce the high rates of exclusionary discipline practices in schools and reduce disparities in suspension and arrest rates by students' race and disability status.[18] At the national release, Secretary of Education Arne Duncan and Attorney General Eric Holder recognized the need to provide a safe, productive school environment, but emphasized concerns that have been raised across the country about the extensive use of exclusionary discipline practices, particularly for students of color and students with disabilities.

In Chicago, there have been a number of district-initiated reforms over the past five years intended to decrease the amount of instructional time lost to exclusionary practices and to improve students' and teachers' feelings of safety at school (**see box Policy Shifts in Chicago Public Schools on p.8**). These policies have included funding for implementing alternative programs for addressing behavioral problems, as well as modifications to the CPS Student Code of Conduct (SCC) to discourage schools from using suspensions and reduce the amount of time students miss school when they are suspended. CPS has adopted a Multi-Tiered System of Supports (MTSS),[19] also known as Response to Intervention (RtI), to help guide the use of various alternative discipline approaches, including the prevention of exclusionary disciplinary practices among all students, targeted supports for students with higher needs, and individualized interventions for the most at-risk students. A number of schools have implemented programs that teach students positive behaviors (e.g., Positive Behavioral Intervention Supports, or PBIS) or that address social-emotional learning needs. For students who are facing disciplinary action, many schools are implementing restorative justice programs, where students are taught to take responsibility and repair harm, rather than simply issuing a suspension or other punishment.

In February 2014, CPS released a plan to reduce the use of exclusionary disciplinary practices in schools called the Suspensions and Expulsions Reduction Plan (SERP). The district gathered stakeholders from across

---

11 Losen & Gillespie (2012); Porowski, O'Conner, & Aikaterini (2014).
12 Fabelo et al. (2011); Finn & Servos (2013); McFarland (2001); Skiba, Horner, Chung, Rausch, May, & Tobin (2011); Skiba, Shure, & Williams (2012); Welch & Payne (2010).
13 Fabelo et al. (2011); Balfanz et al. (2013).
14 Steinberg et al. (2011).
15 Mattison & Amber (2007).
16 American Academy of Pediatrics (2003); American Psychological Association Zero Tolerance Task Force (2008).
17 Alvarez (2013); Kwong (2014); Watanabe (2014).
18 U.S. Department of Education (2014).
19 Chicago Public Schools Office of Social and Emotional Learning (n.d.)

the city, calling the group the Chicago Collaborative for Supportive School Discipline, to hear different perspectives on school disciplinary practices.[20] They also developed new guidelines and training for school leaders to try to address the high rates of exclusionary disciplinary practices in schools.

As CPS schools, their community partners, and parents continue to work on these issues, they need to have a sense of the degree to which exclusionary discipline practices are actually used in schools, why they are used, and how practices have changed over time. This report—the first in a series on discipline practices in CPS—maps out the scope of the issue the district is addressing. This report provides an overview of the use of exclusionary discipline in CPS and the degree to which practices have changed from 2008-09 to 2013-14. It focuses on students in grades 6-12 who are at highest risk of receiving a suspension.[21] This report builds on statistics that have been released previously by the district to provide additional information about the use of disciplinary practices in schools.[22] It provides suspension rates separately for students in the middle and high school grades and shows changes in ISS rates, as well as changes in OSS rates and arrest rates of students in schools. It examines differences across student subgroups, analyzing suspension and arrest rates by race, gender, special education status, and student achievement. This report also provides an analysis of the reasons that students are suspended and draws on interviews with school administrators to highlight some of the issues with which they struggle when trying to maintain discipline in their building. **Appendix A** provides information about the data used for this study **(see also box *Data Sources and Years* on p.9)**. This report addresses the following questions:

- To what extent do CPS schools use exclusionary disciplinary practices, including out-of-school suspensions, in-school suspensions, and police notifications/arrests?

- Have Chicago schools changed their use of exclusionary disciplinary practices from 2008-09 to 2013-14, particularly in years when district policy changes occurred?

- What are the differences in suspension rates across different groups of students (by race, gender, achievement level, and disability status)?

- Why do students receive exclusionary discipline? What types of incidents are most prevalent in schools?

The next chapter presents detailed information about the use of exclusionary discipline practices in CPS from 2008-09 to 2013-14. Chapter 2 examines student behaviors associated with suspensions and police contact. Chapter 3 shows how students and teacher perceptions of safety and discipline issues have changed over time. Finally, the last section considers implications of the report's findings for CPS and other districts looking to reduce the use of exclusionary disciplinary practices.

---

20 Some of the authors of this report participated in some of the meetings of the Chicago Collaborative for Supportive School Discipline to learn about the issues that were brought up from stakeholders, and to provide information about research findings around disciplinary practices in Chicago schools.

21 Losen & Martinez (2013); Skiba & Rausch (2010).
22 CPS released three early reports of discipline trends in 2014. See Chicago Public Schools (2014a, 2014b, 2014c).

Definitions of Key Terms

CPS Student Code of Conduct (SCC): This document outlines what behaviors are inappropriate for students and the appropriate ways for schools to address misbehavior. It is modified annually and parents and students are required to sign the SCC. The most recent version of the SCC is available here: http://cps.edu/Pages/StudentCodeofConduct.aspx

Exclusionary Practices: Practices that result in the removal of students from the classroom, including out-of-school and in-school suspensions, as well as arrests.

Out-of-School Suspension (OSS): A suspension that removes a student from the building for a set number of days.

In-School Suspension (ISS): A suspension that removes a student from the classroom, but not the building. Students often sit in a room designated for in-school suspensions where they are expected to do schoolwork.

Arrests: Chicago Police Department (CPD) data indicate whether a student was arrested, the address at which the student was arrested, and the address at which the incident occurred. These addresses are used to identify whether an arrest was made for an incident that occurred at school or out of school.

Suspension and Arrest Rates: We define rates as the percentage of students who experience a particular exclusionary practice in a given school year. For example, in 2013-14 the OSS rate for high school students was 16 percent—as we define it, this means that 16 percent of high school students received at least one OSS in the 2013-14 school year. Arrest rates only include arrests made during the school year, not during the summer.

Non-Exclusionary Discipline Practices: Practices other than suspensions that seek to change behaviors or offer behavioral supports to students, such as restorative justice practices, counseling, and social-emotional training. While not included in this report, non-exclusionary practices are the focus of future work in this series.

Policy Shifts in Chicago Public Schools

CPS has enacted strategies to reduce the use of exclusionary practices like suspensions. These policies also emphasize the use of behavioral supports for students in lieu of suspensions.

Culture of Calm Initiative (2009-10 and 2010-11): Through the Culture of Calm Initiative, the district provided several high schools with funds to implement programs for addressing behavioral and safety problems. New school-based strategies included peer juries, restorative justice, counseling, and other alternative practices to help students develop better relationships with peers and adults and to improve overall school climate. CPS piloted the initiative in six high schools in 2009-10 and expanded support to nearly 40 high schools in 2010-11.

Changes to the CPS Student Code of Conduct (at the start of the 2012-13 school year): In the fall of 2012, CPS modified its Student Code of Conduct (SCC) to reduce the length of suspensions. The changes in the SCC eliminated automatic 10-day suspensions and required principals to seek district approval to suspend students for more than five days. The new SCC also offered a wide range of options to school administrators. According to the district, these options were intended to provide flexibility to administrators rather than a one-size-fits-all approach to discipline. The amended SCC also recommended using non-exclusionary practices—such as peace circles and mentoring—to resolve conflicts and behavioral issues.

Suspensions and Expulsions Reduction Plan (SERP) (during 2013-14): In February 2013, CPS released a plan to explicitly reduce the use of exclusionary disciplinary practices in schools. They also developed new guidelines and training for school leaders to try to address the high rates of exclusionary disciplinary practices. In June 2014, they further revised the SCC. While these revisions to the SCC would not impact the trends reported here, the activities of the SERP could have encouraged schools to limit the use of out-of-school suspensions.

Data Sources and Years

Data for this report come from a number of sources, including CPS administrative data, CPD arrest records, responses of students and teachers to the My Voice, My School surveys, and interviews of school administrators. Here we describe which sources of data were used for each chapter. Additional information on the data sources is provided in the appendices.

Chapter 1
Trends in Exclusionary Discipline Practices in CPS

Trends in suspension rates are calculated from CPS administrative data from the 2008-09 to 2013-14 school years. These trends do not include students enrolled in charter, alternative, or special education schools, as described in **Appendix A**.

Trends in arrest rates are calculated from CPD data that have been matched with CPS enrollment files from the 2006-07 to 2011-12 school years. These trends do include students in charter schools, but not alternative or special education schools.

Chapter 2
Reasons for Suspensions and Police Involvement

Reasons for out-of school suspensions, in-school suspensions, and arrests are calculated from CPS administrative data for the 2012-13 school year. These analyses do not include students enrolled in charter, alternative, or special education schools.

Administrator concerns about behavioral and disciplinary issues come from interviews with 20 administrators conducted in the spring and summer of 2013.

Chapter 3
Perceptions of School Safety and Order

Trends in student perceptions of safety and teacher perceptions of discipline challenges come from district-wide My Voice, My School surveys from the spring of 2007 and 2009, and every following spring until 2014. Survey responses for individual items highlighted are from the spring 2014 administration. These analyses do not include students enrolled in charter, alternative, or special education schools.

CHAPTER 1

Trends in Exclusionary Discipline Practices in CPS

This chapter examines the use of student suspensions and arrests in CPS before and after the implementation of two major policies: the Culture of Calm Initiative in high schools (2009-10 and 2010-11) and major changes to the CPS Student Code of Conduct (SCC) prior to the 2012-13 school year (see box *Policy Shifts in Chicago Public Schools* on p.8). Both policies attempted to encourage schools to use a broader range of responses to student behavioral problems. We show suspension rates for the 2013-14 school year, track how suspension rates have changed between 2008-09 and 2013-14 during a policy climate focused on reducing suspensions, and examine differences in suspension rates across subgroups of students. We also discuss the changes in the length of suspensions across the same time period. The second half of the chapter looks at student arrests, drawing on Chicago Police Department (CPD) data from 2006-07 to 2011-12.

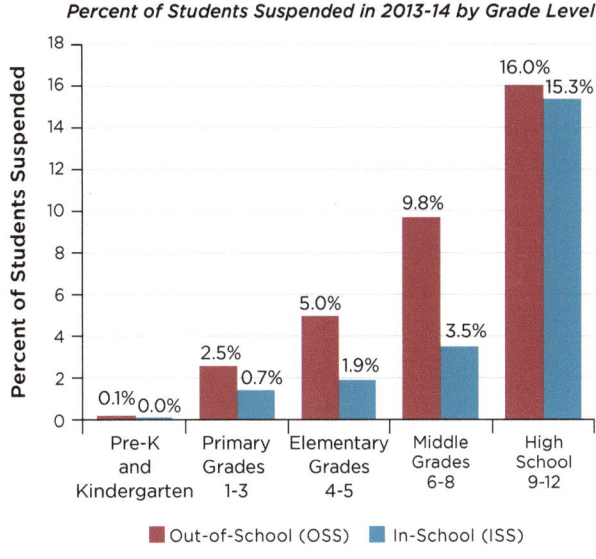

FIGURE 1

Older Students Are More Likely to be Suspended Than Younger Students

Percent of Students Suspended in 2013-14 by Grade Level

Note: Suspensions reported are from 2013-14 CPS administrative data on student misconducts. Students enrolled in charter, alternative, or special education schools are not included in this analysis.

Suspensions

Suspensions are common in CPS, especially in high schools. Suspensions in CPS are not limited to a handful of students, especially at the high school level. About one-quarter of high school students (23 percent) received either an out-of-school suspension (OSS) or in-school suspension (ISS) in the 2013-14 school year. The fact that a quarter of students in high schools are suspended each year suggests that it is not simply a few students with particularly bad disciplinary problems who are being suspended. Sixteen percent of high school students received at least one OSS and about the same percentage received at least one ISS (**see Figure 1**). Suspension rates are lower for middle grade students than high school students, and few middle grade students receive in-school suspensions. Ten percent of students received an OSS in the 2013-14 school year, while 3.5 percent received an ISS.

Students in earlier elementary school grades also receive suspensions; about 8,000 out-of-school suspensions given in the 2013-14 school year were for students below grade six, which is almost 17 percent of all out-of-school suspensions (**see Figure 2**). While this is a large number of suspensions, it is small compared to the number of out-of-school suspensions given to middle school or high school students, who received over 40,000 out-of-school suspensions in the 2013-14 school year. The majority of suspensions in CPS occur in high schools; over half of out-of-school suspensions occur among high school students (56 percent), and the vast majority of in-school suspensions are for high school students (86 percent).

Suspensions in the elementary grades are sometimes viewed as more problematic than suspensions in the high school grades because younger students are viewed as less responsible for their behaviors and more in need of nurturing. However, because the majority of suspensions occur in the high school grades, there cannot be a large reduction in suspension rates in CPS, or

FIGURE 2

Over Half of All Out-of-School Suspensions in CPS were Given to High School Students

Out-of-School Suspensions in 2013-14 by Grade Level

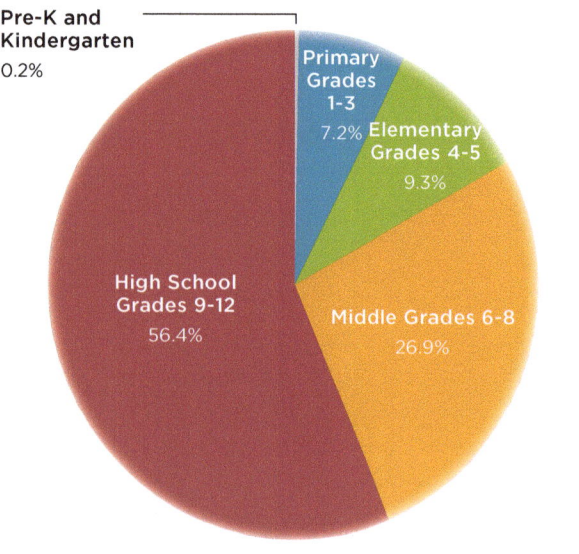

Pre-K and Kindergarten 0.2%
Primary Grades 1-3: 7.2%
Elementary Grades 4-5: 9.3%
Middle Grades 6-8: 26.9%
High School Grades 9-12: 56.4%

Note: Numbers reported are from 2013-14 CPS administrative data. Students enrolled in charter, alternative, or special education schools are not included in this analysis.

a reduction in discipline disparities, without substantial changes in discipline practices in the high schools. Suspensions in higher grade levels may not elicit as much concern, but suspensions mean that students miss class more often. Class attendance is critical in high school and in the middle grades, as it is highly predictive of academic attainment and achievement.[23]

Out-of-school suspension rates have steadily declined in high schools, while in-school suspension rates have increased. OSS rates have slowly declined over time, dropping each year since the 2009-10 school year (**see Figure 3**). The Culture of Calm initiative may have contributed to the steady drop in OSS rates in high school by raising awareness of alternative discipline responses. There do not seem to be dramatic reductions in OSS rates corresponding to the 2012-13 changes to the SCC. However, in 2013-14, the OSS rates dropped 3 percentage points, from 19 percent in 2012-13 to 16 percent at the end of 2013-14.

FIGURE 3

Out-of-School Suspension Rates Declined in 2013-14, but Suspension Rates Remain High Overall

Six Year Trends in Out-of-School and In-School Suspensions

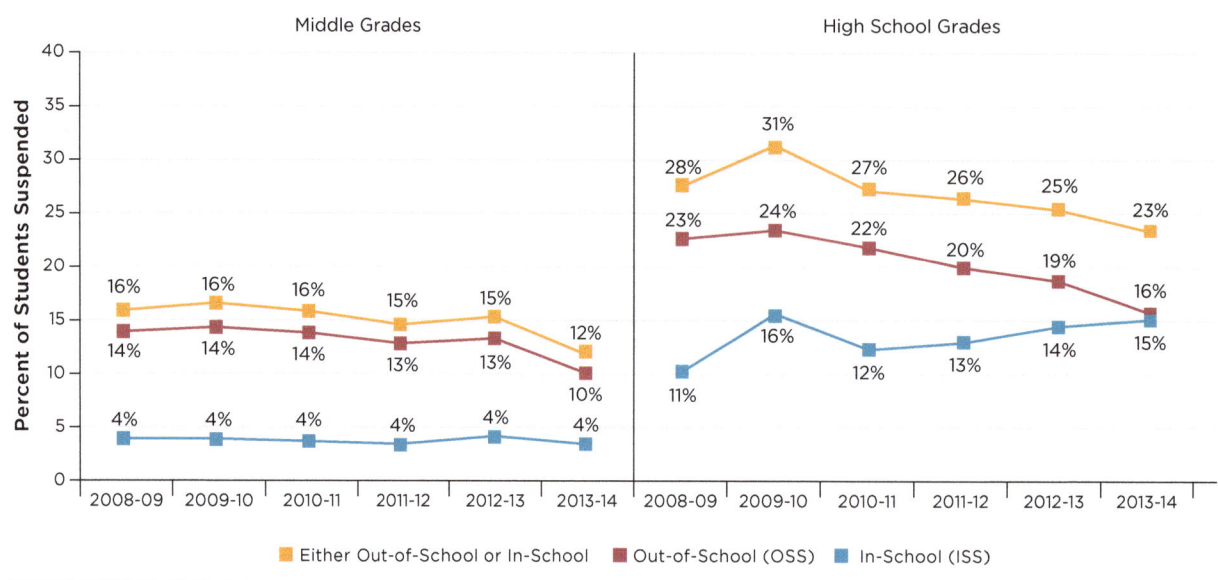

Note: When calculating suspension rates, the numerator is the total number of students assigned at least one suspension in that school year and the denominator is the total student enrollment in the district. Total enrollment is calculated using the number of unique students who are enrolled in the district during the fall and spring semesters. For middle grades, we use only students in grades 6-8 in the calculations, even if the school contains students in other grades. Total suspensions are measured as the percent of students receiving either an OSS or an ISS during the school year. Students who receive both are counted only once in the total suspension rate. Students enrolled in charter schools are not included in the calculations, due to incomplete data.

---

[23] Allensworth & Easton (2007); Neild & Balfanz (2006); Balfanz, Herzog & MacIver (2007); Allensworth, Gwynne, Moore, & de la Torre (2014); Kieffer & Marinell (2012).

During the same period of time, the use of in-school suspensions in high schools has steadily risen from a low of 11 percent in 2008-09 to a high of 15 percent at the end of the 2013-14 school year. As such, the declines in OSS rates have been counterbalanced by the increase in ISS rates.

Out-of-school suspension rates in the middle grades dropped in 2013-14, after five years of little change. In the middle grades, a student's probability of receiving a suspension remained relatively constant from 2008-09 forward, until the 2013-14 school year (see Figure 3). The proportion of students who received at least one suspension during the school year hovered just under 15 percent until it dropped down to 12 percent in 2013-14. ISS rates are very low in the middle grades and have remained below 5 percent for all the years shown in this report. Both OSS and ISS rates in the middle grades in the 2012-13 school year remained similar to prior years, despite changes to the SCC that de-emphasized the use of suspensions in that year.

African American students are more likely to be suspended than students of other racial/ethnic groups. There are significant differences in suspension rates by race and gender in CPS. African American boys receive suspensions at higher rates than any other demographic group. In the 2013-14 school year, 33 percent of African American high school boys received an OSS, compared to 13 percent of Latino boys and 6 percent of white/Asian boys. In the middle grades in the same year, 22 percent of African American boys received at least one OSS—that is about 1-in-5 students (see Figure 4).

African American girls have the second-highest suspension rate; 23 percent of African American high school girls received out-of-school suspensions in the 2013-14 school year, compared to 6 percent of Latina girls and 2 percent of white/Asian girls. In the middle grades, 14 percent of African American girls received an OSS.

Latino boys were much less likely to be suspended than African American students. In high school, 13 percent of Latino boys received an OSS in 2013-14. Eight percent of Latino boys in the middle grades received an OSS.

In-school suspension rates have increased for African American high school students. ISS rates have risen considerably for African American students in high school over the last several years, while remaining fairly constant for other student groups (see Figure 5). The ISS rate for African American boys doubled between 2008-09 and 2013-14—from 15 to 29 percent. Over the same period, ISS rates for African American girls in high school had also doubled from 10 percent to 20 percent. ISS rates for all other student groups remained steady over the last six years, although ISS rates for Latino boys and girls increased slightly in the 2013-14 school year. Thus, the overall increases in CPS high school ISS rates have been driven by African American students.

Students with disabilities are suspended at higher rates than students without disabilities. Students with identified disabilities are more likely to be suspended than students without identified disabilities. At the high school level, almost a quarter of students with disabilities (24 percent) received an OSS in the 2013-14 school year compared with 15 percent of students without identified disabilities (see Figure 6). In the middle grades, 16 percent of students with disabilities received an OSS in the 2013-14 school year, compared to 9 percent of students without identified disabilities Students with disabilities were also more likely to receive in-school suspensions than students without identified disabilities (see Figure 7). As seen in the system-wide trends, OSS rates for students with disabilities have been declining in high schools since the 2009-10 school year, and they declined in the middle grades just in the 2013-14 school year. At the same time, ISS rates for both students with and without identified disabilities in high school have been rising.

Students with low entering test scores are much more likely to be suspended than students with high test scores. One of the student characteristics most strongly related to suspension rates is students' prior achievement. Students with very high test scores—those whose prior test scores put them in the top quartile for their grade—tend to have low suspension rates.

FIGURE 4

African American Students, Particularly Boys, Are More Likely to be Suspended than Other Student Groups, Though Rates Are Declining for All Subgroups

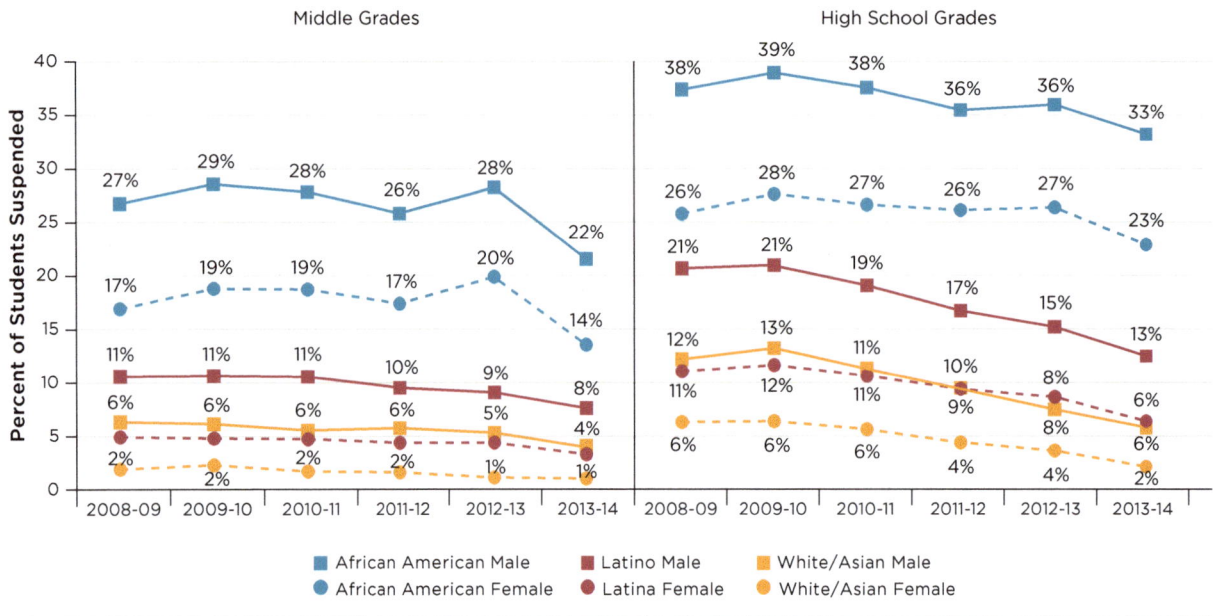

Trends in Out-of-School Suspensions by Race and Gender

Note: When calculating suspension rates, the numerator is the total number of students in the subgroup (i.e., African American males) assigned at least one suspension in that school year and the denominator is the total student subgroup enrollment in the district. Total enrollment is calculated using the number of unique students who are enrolled in the district during the fall and spring semesters. For middle grades, we use only students in grades 6-8 in the calculations, even if the school contains students in other grades. Total suspensions are measured as the percent of students receiving an OSS during the school year. Students enrolled in charter schools are not included in the calculations, due to incomplete data.

FIGURE 5

In-School Suspension Rates Have Increased Primarily for African American High School Students

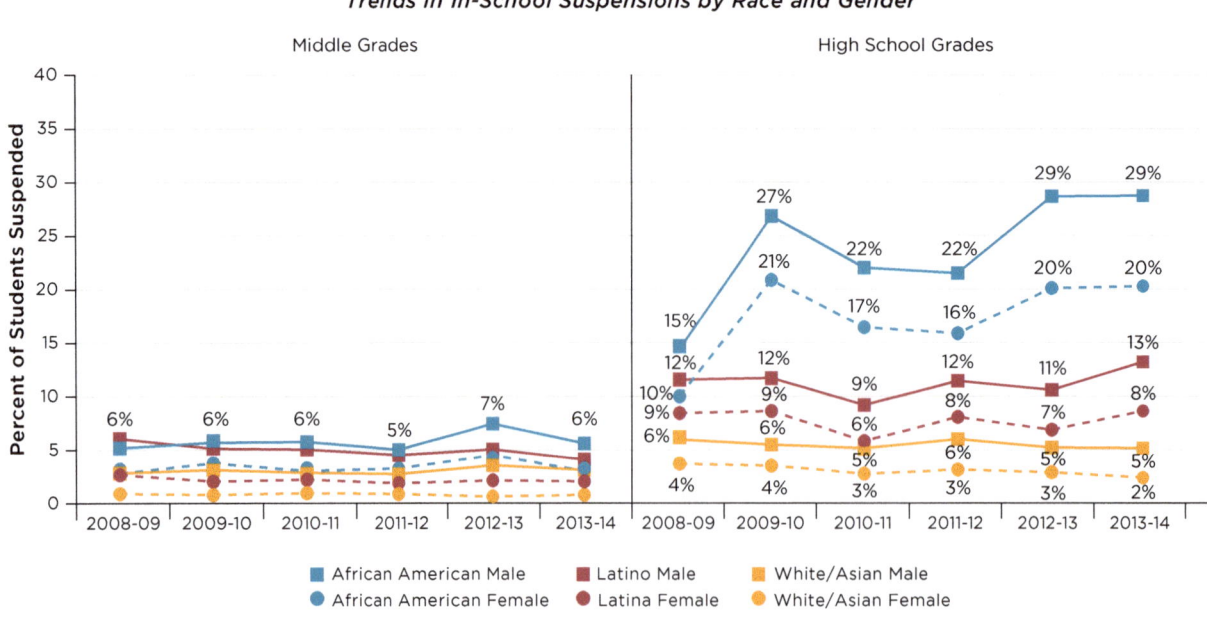

Trends in In-School Suspensions by Race and Gender

Note: When calculating suspension rates, the numerator is the total number of students in the subgroup (i.e., African American males) assigned at least one suspension in that school year and the denominator is the total student subgroup enrollment in the district. Total enrollment is calculated using the number of unique students who are enrolled in the district during the fall and spring semesters. For middle grades, we use only students in grades 6-8 in the calculations, even if the school contains students in other grades. Total suspensions are measured as the percent of students receiving ISS during the school year. Students enrolled in charter schools are not included in the calculations, due to incomplete data.

FIGURE 6

Out-Of-School Suspension Rates Have Been Declining for Students with Disabilities, though They Are Suspended at Higher Rates than Students without Disabilities

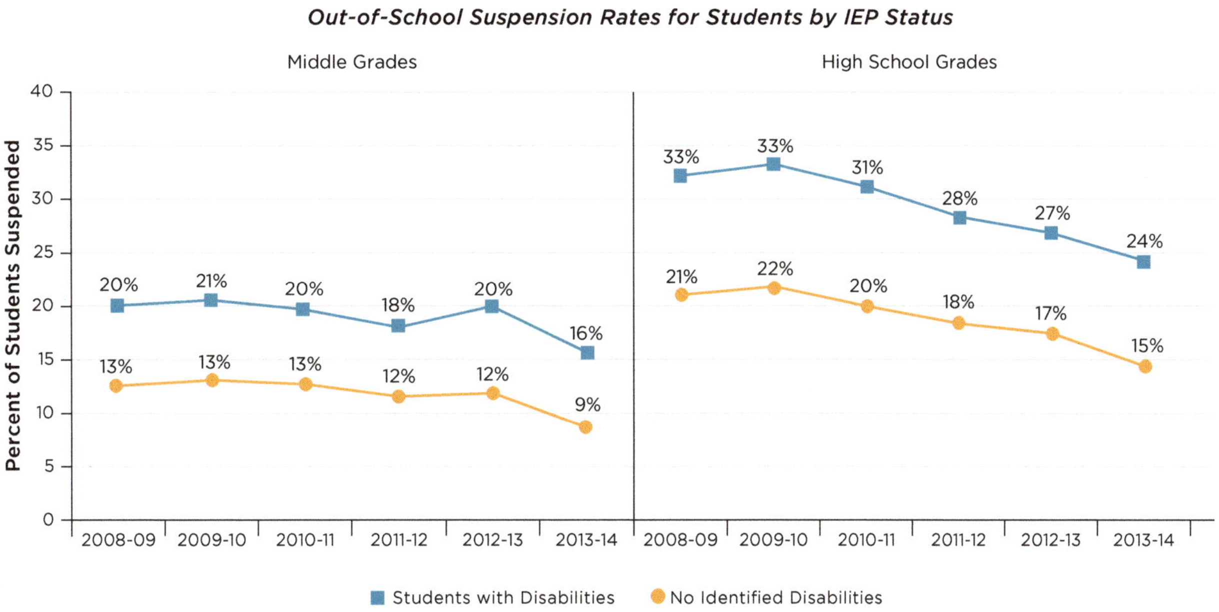

Out-of-School Suspension Rates for Students by IEP Status

Middle Grades

Year	Students with Disabilities	No Identified Disabilities
2008-09	20%	13%
2009-10	21%	13%
2010-11	20%	13%
2011-12	18%	12%
2012-13	20%	12%
2013-14	16%	9%

High School Grades

Year	Students with Disabilities	No Identified Disabilities
2008-09	33%	21%
2009-10	33%	22%
2010-11	31%	20%
2011-12	28%	18%
2012-13	27%	17%
2013-14	24%	15%

Note: When calculating suspension rates, the numerator is the total number of students in the subgroup (i.e., high school students with disabilities) assigned at least one suspension in that school year and the denominator is the total student subgroup enrollment in the district. Total enrollment is calculated using the number of unique students who are enrolled in the district during the fall and spring semesters. For middle grades, we use only students in grades 6-8 in the calculations, even if the school contains students in other grades. Total suspensions are measured as the percent of students receiving an OSS during the school year. Students enrolled in charter schools are not included in the calculations, due to incomplete data.

FIGURE 7

In-School Suspension Rates Have Been Increasing for All High School Students, though Students with Disabilities are Suspended More Often than Students without Disabilities

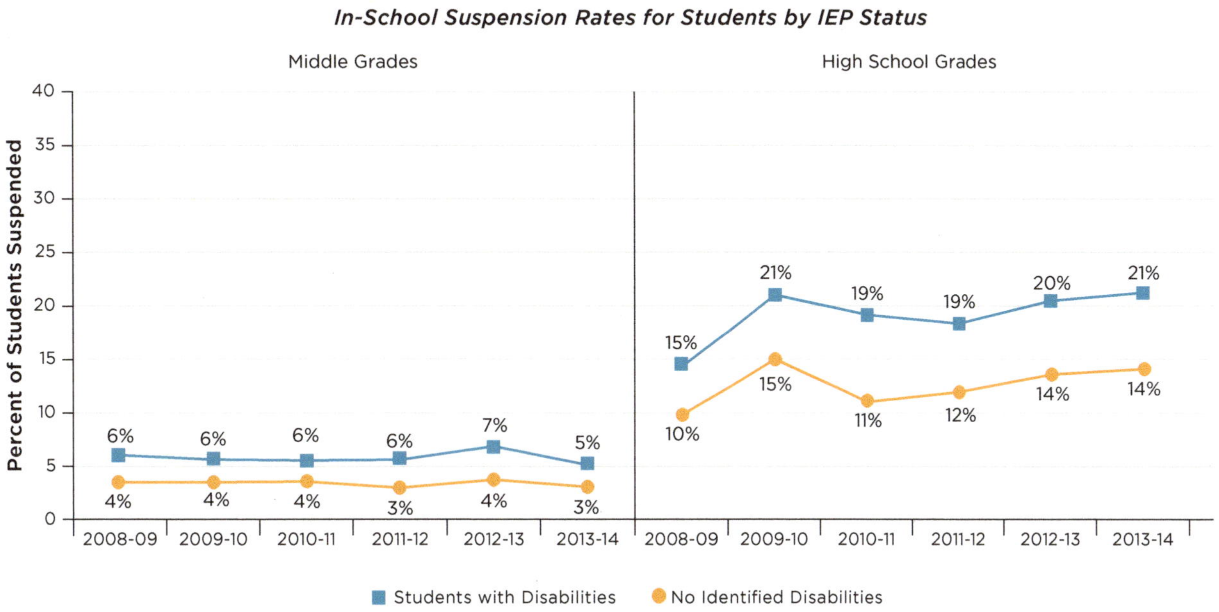

In-School Suspension Rates for Students by IEP Status

Middle Grades

Year	Students with Disabilities	No Identified Disabilities
2008-09	6%	4%
2009-10	6%	4%
2010-11	6%	4%
2011-12	6%	3%
2012-13	7%	4%
2013-14	5%	3%

High School Grades

Year	Students with Disabilities	No Identified Disabilities
2008-09	15%	10%
2009-10	21%	15%
2010-11	19%	11%
2011-12	19%	12%
2012-13	20%	14%
2013-14	21%	14%

Note: When calculating suspension rates, the numerator is the total number of students in the subgroup (i.e., high school students with disabilities) assigned at least one suspension in that school year and the denominator is the total student subgroup enrollment in the district. Total enrollment is calculated using the number of unique students who are enrolled in the district during the fall and spring semesters. For middle grades, we use only students in grades 6-8 in the calculations, even if the school contains students in other grades. Total suspensions are measured as the percent of students receiving ISS during the school year. Students enrolled in charter schools are not included in the calculations, due to incomplete data.

In high school, 7 percent of students with the highest test scores received an OSS in the 2013-14 school year, and 6 percent received an ISS (see Figures 8 and 9). In contrast, students with test scores in the bottom quartile for their grade tend to have very high suspension rates. About a quarter of high school students with the lowest incoming test scores received an OSS and about a quarter received an ISS in the 2013-14 school year. The same patterns can be seen at the middle grades level, with low-achieving students receiving out-of-school suspensions at rates that are five times higher than students with high prior achievement (see Figures 8 and 9). Students who start out the year with achievement that is behind their grade-level peers are particularly likely to receive discipline that takes them out of the classroom. This is of particular concern because prior research has shown that absences from middle school are strongly predictive of later educational outcomes, including students' grades and pass rates, high school graduation, and college readiness.[24] Even just a few days of absence can substantially lower students' likelihood of later academic attainment.

The length of suspensions has declined. The length of time for which students are missing school due to suspensions has been declining over time. In high schools, the average OSS length was 3.4 days long in 2008-09 (see Figure 10). The average length of suspensions declined very slightly each year, until the 2013-14 school year when the average OSS length decreased dramatically to 2.7 days. In 2008-09, a typical OSS resulted in a student missing just under three days in the middle grades, on average; by 2013-14, the average OSS length was 2.4 days for a single suspension. While not shown in a figure, African American boys and girls receive the longest suspensions per incident, on average, but their suspensions lengths have been declining along with other student groups. The biggest drop occurred in 2012-13, when the average length of an OSS for African American boys in high school dropped by 0.5 days.

The reduction in OSS length coincides with the year that the new SCC went into effect in CPS (the 2012-13 school year); the policy explicitly constrained the use of long suspensions—any suspension longer than five days had to be approved by central office personnel. While the policy was in effect for both elementary and high schools, high school students were more likely to be affected by the policy because long suspensions are much more common at the high school level. In fact, 39 percent of schools serving the middle grades did not give any long suspensions in the 2011-12 school year, so this policy change did not affect them. At the same time, all but one high school did give long suspensions prior to the policy.

While the length of OSS has decreased over time, the length of ISS in the middle and high school grades has stayed fairly stable at 1.5 days for all student groups (see Figure 10). When disaggregated by student groups, ISS lengths have gotten shorter for African American students, but they have gotten slightly longer or remained the same length for other student groups. Thus, while African American students have become more likely to receive an ISS in more recent years, the length of those suspensions has declined, on average. (Not shown in a figure.)

---

[24] Allensworth & Easton (2007); Allensworth, Gwynne, Moore, & de la Torre (2014).

FIGURE 8

Students with Lower Incoming Achievement Are More Likely to be Suspended

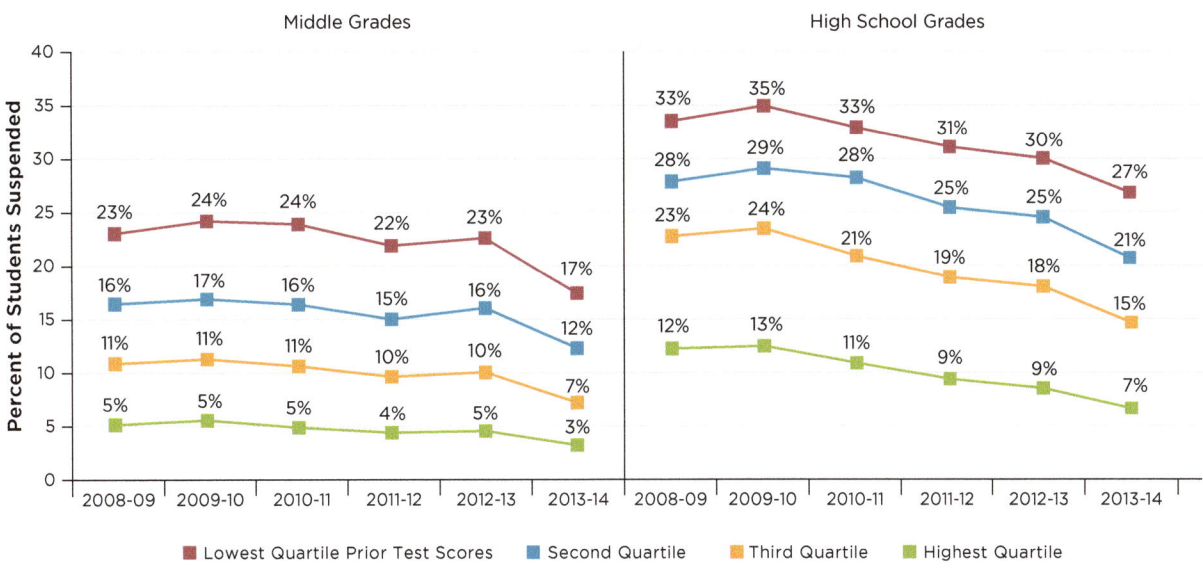

Trends in Out-of-School Suspensions by Students' Prior Test Scores

Note: When calculating suspension rates, the numerator is the total number of students in the subgroup (i.e., high school students in the lowest quartile of prior test scores) assigned at least one suspension in that school year and the denominator is the total student subgroup enrollment in the district. Total enrollment is calculated using the number of unique students who are enrolled in the district during the fall and spring semesters. For middle grades, we use only students in grades 6-8 in the calculations, even if the school contains students in other grades. Total suspensions are measured as the percent of students receiving an OSS during the school year. Students enrolled in charter schools are not included in the calculations, due to incomplete data.

FIGURE 9

Increases in In-School Suspension Rates are Driven by High School Students with Low Achievement

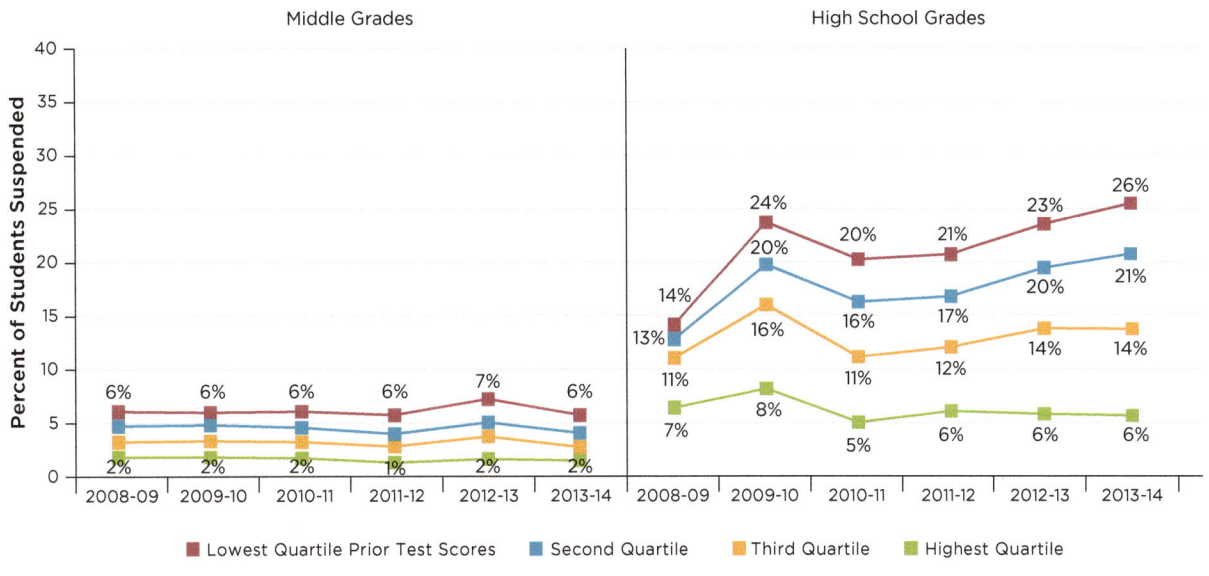

Trends in In-School Suspensions by Students' Prior Test Scores

Note: When calculating suspension rates, the numerator is the total number of students in the subgroup (i.e., high school students in the lowest quartile of prior test scores) assigned at least one suspension in that year and the denominator is the total student subgroup enrollment in the district. Total enrollment is calculated using the number of unique students who are enrolled in the district during the fall and spring semesters. For middle grades, we use only students in grades 6-8 in the calculations, even if the school contains students in other grades. Total suspensions are measured as the percent of students receiving ISS during the school year. Students enrolled in charter schools are not included in the calculations, due to incomplete data.

FIGURE 10

The Length of Out-of-School Suspensions Has Declined Over Time

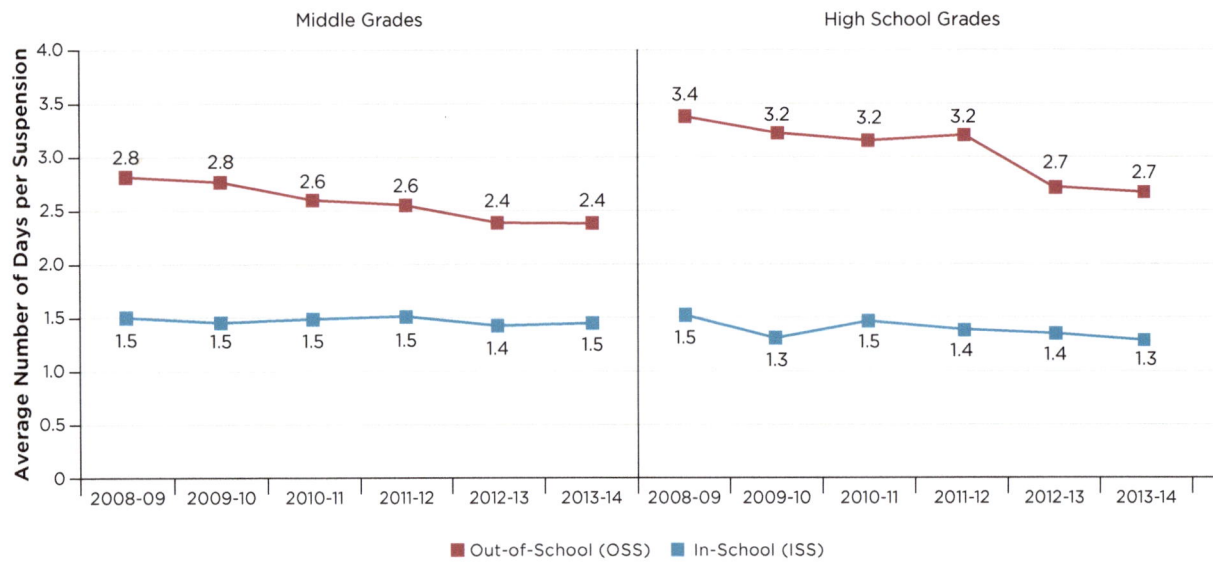

Average Length of Suspensions

Note: Suspension length is calculated by dividing the total days students were suspended in the district by the total number of times suspensions were assigned. For middle grades, we use only students in grades 6-8 in the calculations, even if the school contains students in other grades. Students enrolled in charter schools are not included in the calculations, due to incomplete data.

Arrests

Student arrest rates have declined each year. Arrests of youth enrolled in grades 6-12 in Chicago have been declining over time **(see Figure 11)**. We look at trends in two types of arrests—arrests for at-school incidents and arrests for incidents that happened outside of school. Prior to the 2010-11 school year, just over 2 percent of high school students and just under 1 percent of middle grade students were arrested at school each year for incidents that occurred at school. These arrest rates for in-school incidents remained fairly steady through school year 2009-10, but declined slightly over the next two years. By the 2011-12 school year, the percentage of students arrested for incidents occurring at school had declined from 2.4 percent of high school students in 2009-10 to 1.8 percent of high school students in 2011-12, and from 0.8 percent of middle grade students in 2009-10 to 0.5 percent of middle grade students in 2011-12.

Trends in arrests of CPS students for out-of-school incidents declined even more than arrests for incidents occurring at school. Arrests for events occurring outside of school have been declining since 2007, while arrests for in-school incidents have only been declining since 2010. Still, more students are arrested for incidents occurring outside of school than in school; 4.3 percent of high school students were arrested in 2011-12 for events occurring outside of school. This was down from 5.7 percent of high school students in 2006-07. Arrests for incidents outside of school have also declined among students enrolled in the middle grades; from 1.9 percent in 2006-07 to 1.1 percent in 2011-12. Thus, fewer students enrolled in grades 6-12 are being arrested, and the declines are largely being driven by changes occurring outside of school. Most students who are arrested at school are only arrested once in a year—91 percent of high school students and 94 percent of middle grade students in 2011-12 who were arrested had only one arrest that school year.

African American boys are more likely to be arrested than other high school students. As with suspensions, African American boys are far more likely to be arrested for a school-based incident than any other student subgroup **(see Figure 12**—note that this figure shows only arrests for incidents that occurred at school). In fact, before the 2010-11 school year, about

FIGURE 11

Arrest Rates Have Gone Down over Time, Especially in High Schools After 2009

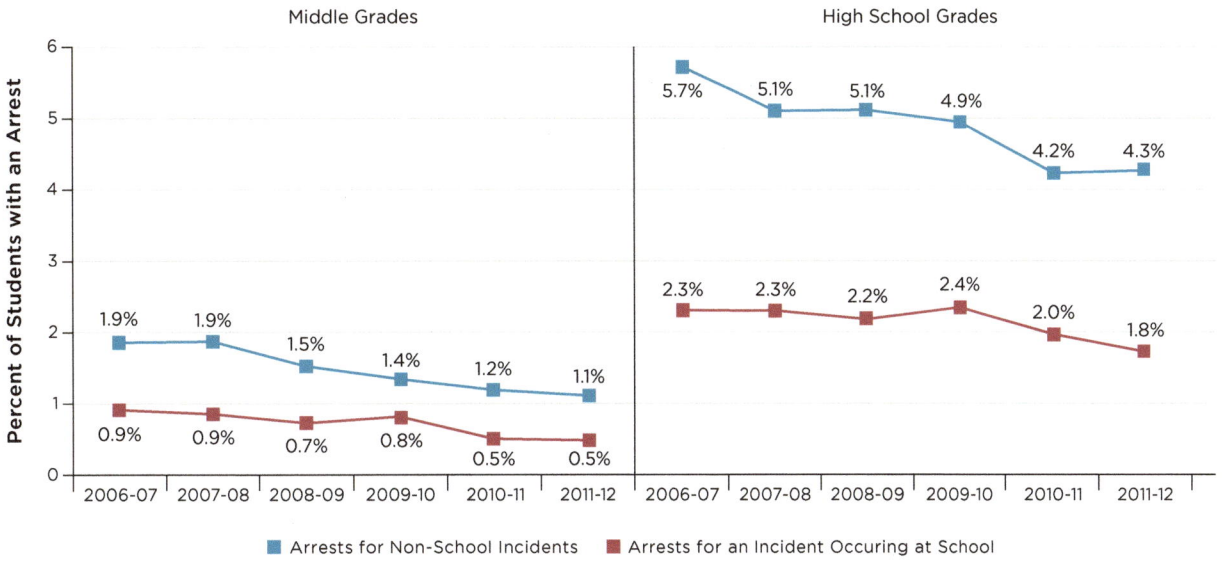

Percentage of Students Arrested during the School Year

Note: When calculating arrest rates, the numerator is the total number of students with at least one arrest in that school year and the denominator is the total student enrollment. Only youth actively enrolled in CPS schools are included in either number. Arrest rates include students in both charter and regular CPS schools, but not students in alternative or special education schools. A student with arrests for both an incident occurring at school and an incident occurring outside of school during the school year would be counted in both categories. Arrest rates are calculated using Chicago Police Department administrative data.

one out of every 20 African American male students in high school was arrested at school during the year. African American male students continue to have the highest arrest rates of any other demographic subgroup of students; but the sharpest decline in arrest rates in the most recent years has occurred among African American boys, falling from 4.8 percent to 3.6 percent. Notably, this sharp decline in arrest rates occurs after the Culture of Calm implementation in CPS high schools. Arrest rates also declined for Latino and white boys during the same period, but to a lesser extent. Two percent of African American girls and Latino boys are arrested for events at school, compared to 1 percent or less among white/Asian students or Latina girls.

FIGURE 12

African American Males Are More Likely to be Arrested than Other Student Groups, but also Show the Largest Decline in Arrest Rates after 2009

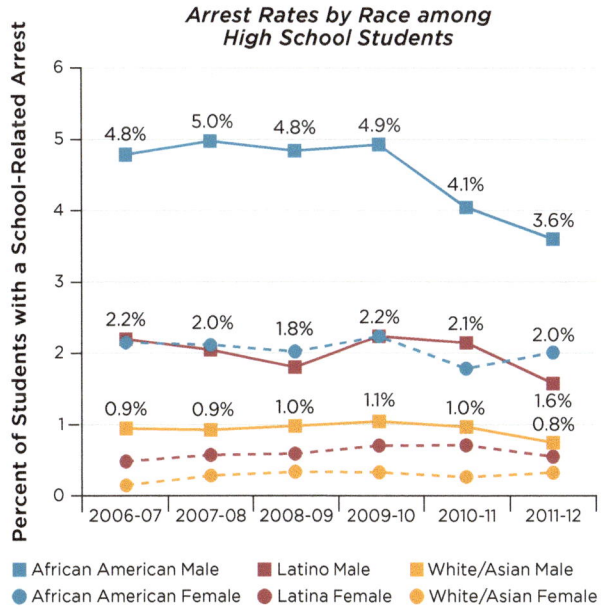

Note: When calculating arrest rates, the numerator is the total number of students in the subgroup (i.e., African American males) with an arrest for an incident occurring at school in that school year and the denominator is the total student subgroup enrollment in the district. Total enrollment is calculated using the number of unique students who are enrolled in the district during the fall and spring semesters. Arrest rates include students in both charter and regular CPS schools, but not students in alternative or special education schools.

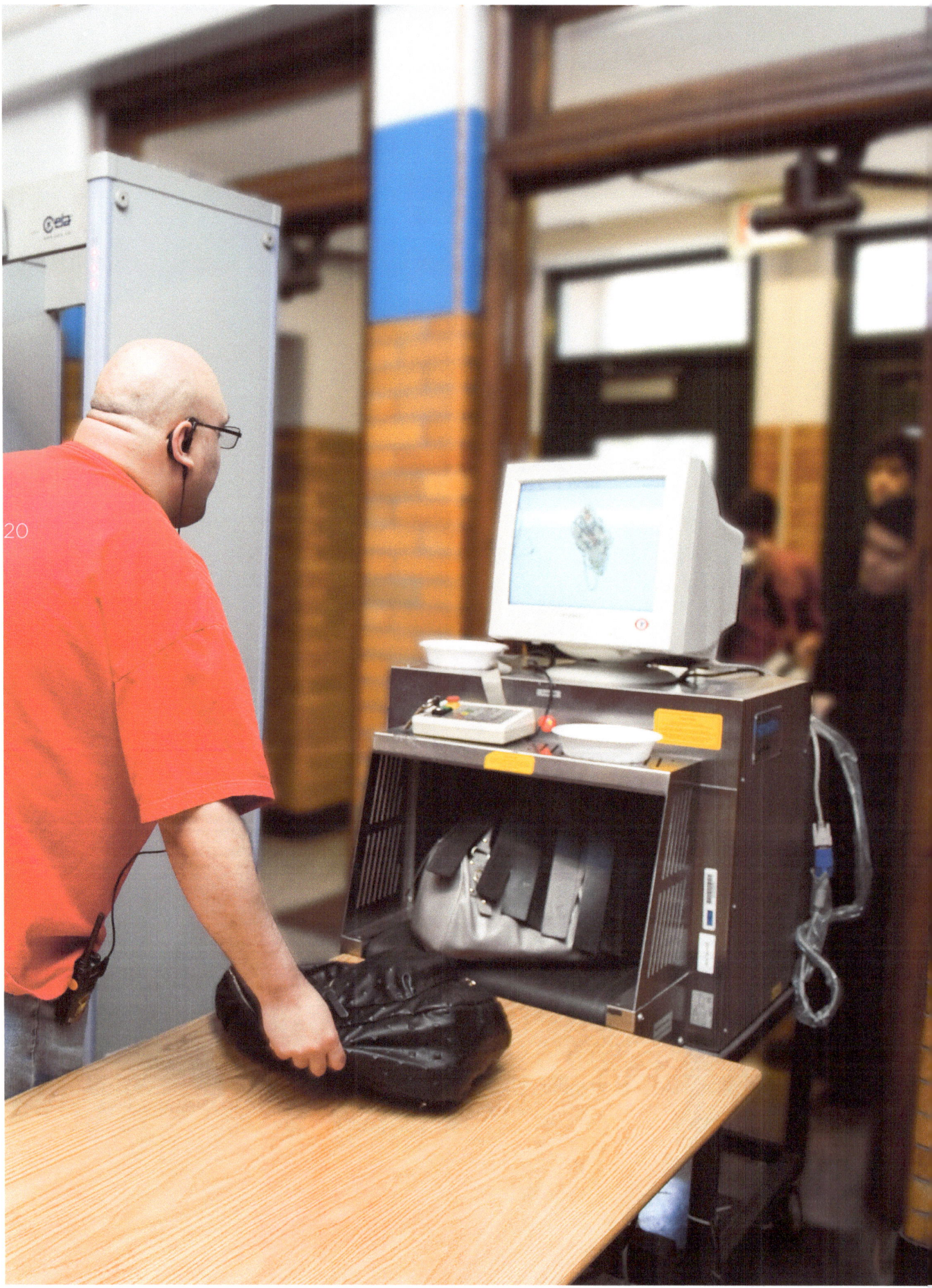

CHAPTER 2

Reasons for Suspensions and Police Involvement

The suspensions and arrests described in the previous chapter are in response to the variety of behavioral challenges faced by school leaders and educators, ranging from minor infractions, like running in the halls, to very severe incidents, such as aggravated assault. Knowing which behaviors lead to suspensions can help districts provide target supports for addressing problem areas and develop policies for leveraging specific opportunities for improvements.

School staff record instances of student misbehavior using a list of infractions in the CPS Student Code of Conduct (SCC). Each recorded incident is placed on a scale of 1 (minor infractions, such as running in the halls) to 6 (very serious infractions, such as arson or attempted murder). Within each group, infractions are given an additional code denoting the exact nature of the infraction (e.g., *"Leaving class without permission"*). In total, the SCC identifies 216 possible infractions. Finally, schools also record the actions taken in response to the infraction, including whether the student received an in-school (ISS) or out-of-school suspension (OSS).

In this chapter, we split the SCC infractions into three main categories (**see Appendix B** for more information on our classification). The first category of behaviors is *Defiance and Violations of School Rules*, which includes infractions that do not threaten the physical safety of students or adults. Rather, they disrupt the learning environment and school processes, or they challenge the authority of adults. The second category of behaviors is *Conflict and Threats to Safety,* which captures various levels of physical altercations and threats between students or between adults and students. These behaviors directly jeopardize the safety of people in the school building. The third category of behaviors is *Illegal Behaviors*, which includes cases of possession or distribution of illegal substances, technology violations, and acts of theft or vandalism. While serious and illegal, these behaviors do not directly compromise the safety of individuals or the school community (**see Table 1**).

TABLE 1
Types of Behavioral Infractions

Behavior Categories	Behavior Groups
Defiance and Violations of School Rules	■ Defiance of School Staff ■ Disruptive Behaviors ■ Miscellaneous School Rule Violations ■ Attendance/Truancy
Conflict and Threats to Safety	■ Physical Altercations ■ Bullying/Intimidation ■ Weapons Violations ■ Sexual Assault
Illegal Behaviors	■ Illegal Substances ■ Technology Violations ■ Theft/Vandalism

Note: UChicago CCSR categorization of infractions in the 2012-13 CPS SCC.

We begin by looking at the reasons students receive suspensions and how administrators describe common problems in their schools, and we then discuss police involvement.

Suspensions

Defiance of adults and school rules accounts for more suspensions than any other type of behavior.
Student defiance of adult authority and general school rule violations are the most common type of offence leading to suspensions. At the high school level, 62 percent of out-of-school suspensions and 87 percent of in-school suspensions are a result of defiance of adults, disruption, or breaking school rules (**see Figures 13 and 14**). In the middle grades, about half of out-of-school suspensions (53 percent) and 62 percent of in-school suspensions are a result of these types of behaviors. Within this category of behaviors, defiance of adults is the single most common cause of suspensions; in high schools, this behavior accounts for 27 percent of out-of-school suspensions and 24 percent of in-school suspensions. In the middle grades, 27 percent of out-of-school suspensions and 25 percent of in-school suspensions are due to defiance infractions.

In interviews, school administrators describe defiance as students refusing to comply with adult requests or *"talking back"* to adults using inappropriate language. The quotes below illustrate common behaviors witnessed by administrators:

> We have kids that act out, a lot of freshmen. 'I don't want to be in here,' 'I'm not reading today,' 'I'm not doing no work,' 'I'm not going to do nothing,' 'Shut up, stop talking to me.' You know, that's resistance.

> Levels of respect towards adults [is a challenge]. For example, the way students respond to questions, where students always have to respond back when they are reprimanded, or always needing to get the last word in. There's no sense of decorum in the way that [students] present [themselves] in being corrected.

In both the middle grades and high school, conflicts and threats to safety account for less than half of all suspensions. Despite common assumptions that school suspensions are primarily driven by serious infractions like fighting, weapon use, and gang activity, 27 percent of the out-of-school suspensions and 7 percent of the in-school suspensions in high schools are for physical conflicts or other threats to safety (**see Figures 13 and 14**). In the middle grades, where fewer students receive suspensions, threats to safety account for a larger percentage of suspensions, but still less than half—41 percent for out-of-school suspensions and 32 percent for in-school suspensions.

When an incident involves a threat to physical safety, it is usually for fighting or bullying. In high school, about one quarter of out-of-school suspensions (26 percent) result from fighting and bullying. At the middle grades level, fighting and bullying account for 38 percent of the out-of-school suspensions.

Administrators noted that student conflict is particularly challenging because of the impact it can have on others in the building. For example, fights can easily get out of control and lead to chaotic situations. *"Say there's a verbal altercation in the lunchroom,"* one administrator

FIGURE 13

Most Out-of-School Suspensions Are the Result of Acts of Defiance, Followed by Physical Altercations Between Students

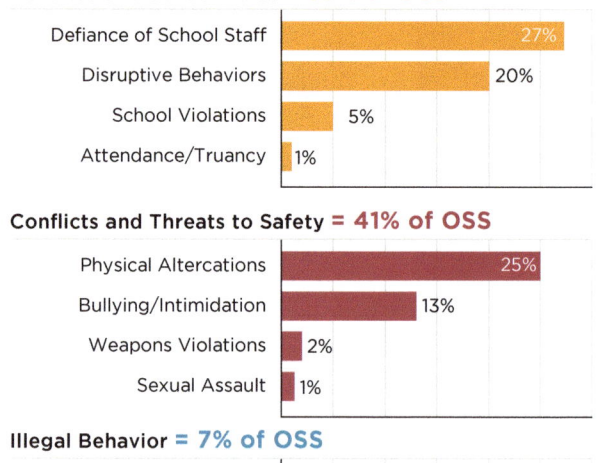

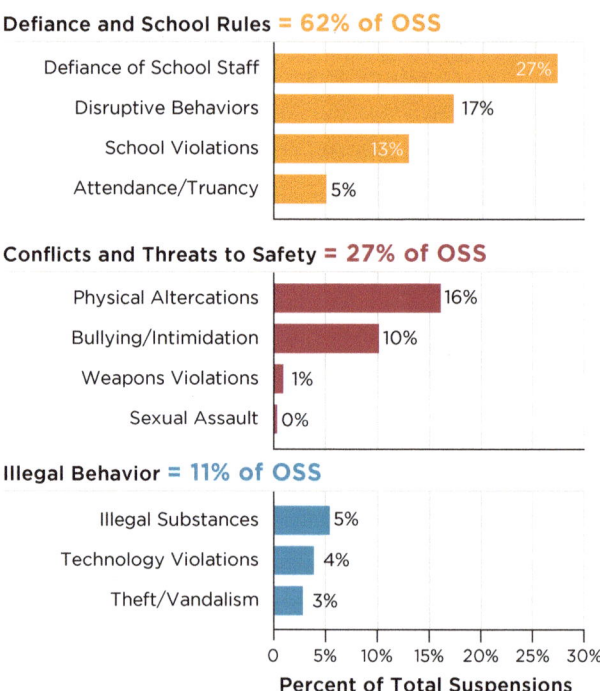

Note: When an incident occurs, schools record the suspension and the reason for the suspension. This figure is an accounting of the reasons for suspensions when a student is assigned a suspension. Numbers reported are from 2012-13 administrative data. Suspensions of students enrolled in charter, alternative, or special education schools are not included in this analysis.

FIGURE 14

Most In-School Suspensions Result from Defiance of Adults and School Rules

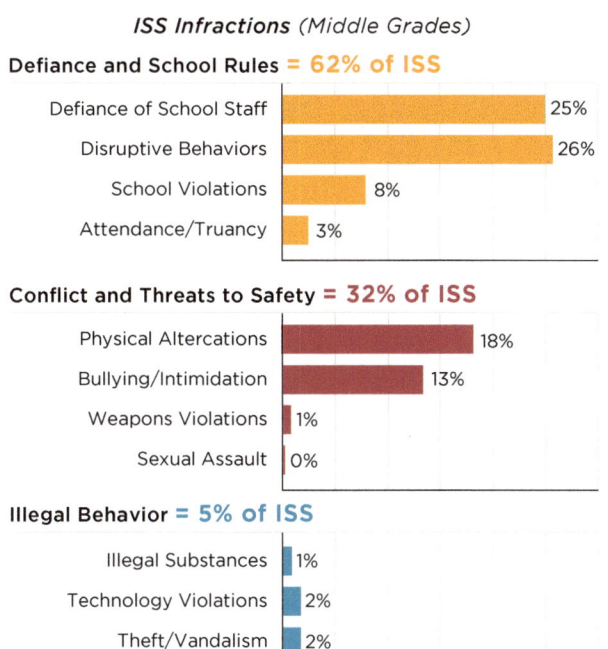

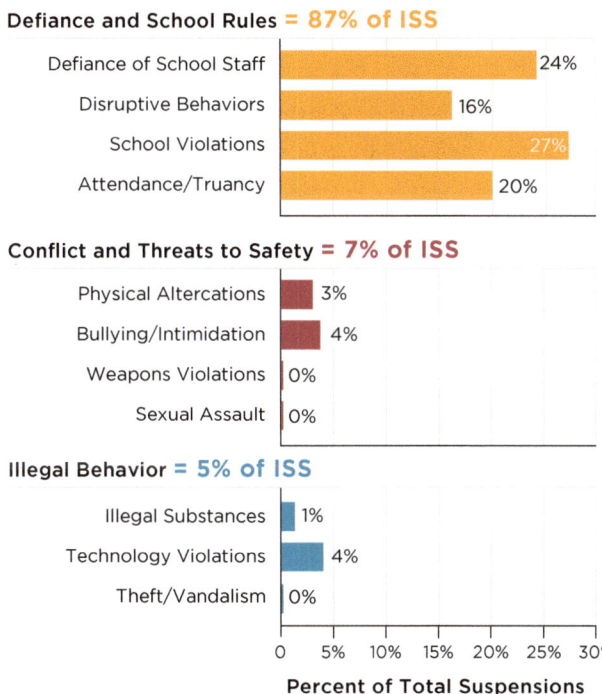

Note: When an incident occurs, schools record the suspension and the reason for the suspension. This figure is an accounting of the reasons for suspensions when a student is assigned a suspension. Numbers reported are from 2012-13 administrative data. Suspensions of students enrolled in charter, alternative, or special education schools are not included in this analysis.

Chapter 2 | Reasons for Suspensions and Police Involvement

explained. *"Every kid in the lunchroom is getting up and trying to go watch a potential fight. To me, that's one of the most important things as far as climate is concerned."*

Pervasive student conflict can also weaken students' connection to school. *"When students see fighting every day, they can say, 'I don't want to go to school today, because who knows what could happen,'"* an administrator reported. By reducing fights, they believed that students would be able to concentrate on learning and would want to be in the school building.

According to some administrators, conflicts are generally the result of limited social-emotional skills of students. *"Many of our students do not know how to socialize in a positive sense; that's why we see a lot of fights,"* one principal explained. *"The biggest problem we have is [teaching] students to be socially responsible and understand how to either talk to adults or talk to their peers in a positive, educational way."* Administrators witness students using profanity, slurs, and other put-downs as a routine part of their interactions. One assistant dean characterized cursing as natural as *"breathing to kids now. 'Okay, good morning, [expletive].' They greet each other vulgarly."*

Another principal said that students can feel compelled by their peers to address disrespect:

> If you're 14 or 15 and you're in the lunchroom, and your friends say, "That girl over there doesn't like you, we heard her saying she didn't like you," well, to buy into the peer pressure, that person has to approach her, or defend their own position.

A number of administrators expressed hope that giving students skills and tools to resolve their differences would prevent verbal and physical fights from escalating. *"[If we can] just figure out a way for our students to be socially responsible, solve their own problems, or talk with somebody, the majority of problems will go away,"* one person reasoned. *"That is the underlying problem that we have."*

High schools routinely use in-school suspensions in response to minor behavioral problems. High schools frequently issue in-school suspensions for violations of general schools rules and attendance issues, as well as defiance and disruption (see Figure 14). In-school suspensions are rarely used for threats to school safety or for illegal behavior. Just over half of the 10 high school administrators we interviewed described regularly responding to minor infractions—such as uniform violations or being late for class—with in-school suspensions. None of the 10 middle school administrators used this approach.

When asked what happens to students who show up to school out of uniform, one high school dean replied:

> If they don't have their uniform, students have to sit an in-school suspension. Automatic. You have to have your dress code, your uniform on. There have been some exceptions, but if they just didn't feel like wearing their uniform they don't have the assets to go to class.

Another administrator said behaviors that would trigger an ISS at their school included:

> Not going to class on time, tardy to class too many times, or calling somebody a '[expletive]' for no apparent reason. Things that we try to change, small behavior that leads to a bigger one. Those are the things that can quickly get you to in-school suspension.

These comments highlight how administrators may issue in-school suspensions as a strategy for reducing common and minor behavior issues.

Some administrators also view ISS as beneficial for students and school culture more generally. The theory is that responding strongly to minor infractions reduces the chance of students engaging in more serious behavior in the future. For example, one dean described a situation where suspension can be used as a proactive response to students' emotional needs:

> If a student is having a rough day, rough situation, we get them out of the population. We like to get them back into the school community that day, but oftentimes that's not logical, because during the early part of the day we saw things going on that if we let them out there they're fighting. Someone's going to say something insensitive to what's going on with them, and their coping skills aren't the greatest, and they're in a really bad mood. So this is a nurturing spot, a lot of times it keeps them away from other things, and we find that method to be very helpful.

By putting students dealing with challenging emotions into an ISS, this dean believes he is protecting students from potentially more serious conflict with their peers. This is a strategy the school uses to support students who may have limited skills for managing emotional stress.

Police Involvement

Even very severe infractions usually do not result in police involvement. The SCC specifies which incidents require schools to contact police, which allow discretion in whether or not to contact police, and which do not warrant police involvement. For example, in the case of battery with no resulting physical injury, the SCC says schools may contact police; but if the battery results in physical injury, schools must contact police. Other infractions that may or must include police involvement include theft, drugs possession, and sexual misconduct. (For a full list of infractions for which schools may or must contact police, **see Appendix C.**)

Even when students engage in behavior for which the SCC recommends or requires police notification, schools usually do not involve police in these reported incidents. **Figure 15** shows the rate of police involvement for incidents involving students in grades 6-12 by SCC recommendations for police notification. Only about 3 percent of incidents for which police involvement is not recommended or required result in police notification, and even fewer result in arrest; this indicates that schools are generally not involving police when it is recommended that they not notify police. For incidents where the SCC specifies that police may be notified, police notification occurs only 22 percent of the time, or for 1-in-5 of these incidents, and arrest occurs about 10 percent of the time.

FIGURE 15

Even When the CPS Code of Conduct Requires Police Contact, Schools Often Do Not Notify Police

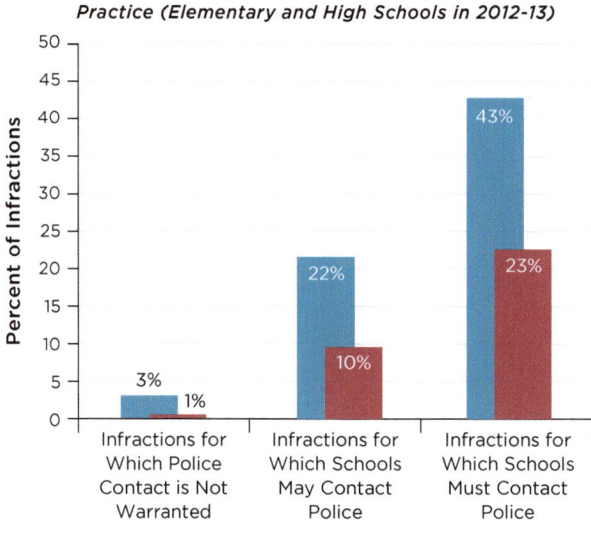

Rates of Police Response and Arrests by Recommended Practice (Elementary and High Schools in 2012-13)

Note: This figure shows the rate of actual police response to infractions occurring across all schools based on whether—and how explicitly—police notification was recommended by the 2012-13 CPS Code of Conduct for that given infraction type. These calculations are based on school administrative data on student misconduct. Police are assumed to have been notified for a reported infraction whenever a police arrest was made. The percentage of infractions for which there were arrests is a subset of the percentage for which police were notified—as indicated by the overlaid arrest bar. The sample of infractions used in these calculations is limited to infractions in CPS groups 3-6 for students in grades 6-12.

For incidents in which the SCC mandates police contact, the police notification rate is slightly over 40 percent. A little more than 20 percent of these infractions result in arrest. These patterns suggest that schools do not always contact police, even when police contact is mandated.

Most police notifications and student arrests are for physical altercations among students. Schools notify police most frequently for physical altercations among students. **Figure 16** shows the total number of notifications and arrests made for infractions that involved students in grades 6-12. Almost 2,500 calls to police were made for instances of physical altercation, resulting in approximately 1,200 arrests. In interviews, school administrators noted they typically did not contact police for one-on-one fights, but for more severe conflicts that might involve multiple people, gangs, weapons, battery, or injury. Physical altercations led to three times more notifications and arrests than the possession or use of illegal substances, the second most responded to incident.

Substance and weapons possession are most likely to prompt police notification when they occur, but they occur infrequently. While substance abuse or possession resulted in many fewer arrests than physical altercations, when it did occur this type of infraction was most likely to prompt a call to police. **Figure 17** shows the rates of police response—both of notification and arrest—by type of infraction. Police notification rates are highest for infractions related to substance abuse; police are called in for more than three out of 10 of these incidents, and they result in arrests 14 percent of the time. In interviews, some school administrators reported that their schools have zero-tolerance policies. In these schools, they automatically call police whenever any illegal substance is confiscated from students. At other schools, administrators said they notify police only if a student is in possession of a large quantify of drugs or is suspected of selling them.

Other types of illegal behavior at school—such as weapons, vandalism, and theft—make up only a very small percentage of arrests or police notifications at schools (**see Figure 16**). Schools are more likely to notify the police for an infraction if it involves a weapon, theft, or vandalism than if it simply involves a physical fight (**see Figure 17**), but these types of infractions are much more rare than physical altercations.

FIGURE 16

Police Are Far More Likely to be Notified and Make Arrests for Peer Conflicts than Any Other Type of Infraction

Total Number of Police Responses by Type of Infraction (Elementary and High Schools in 2012-13)

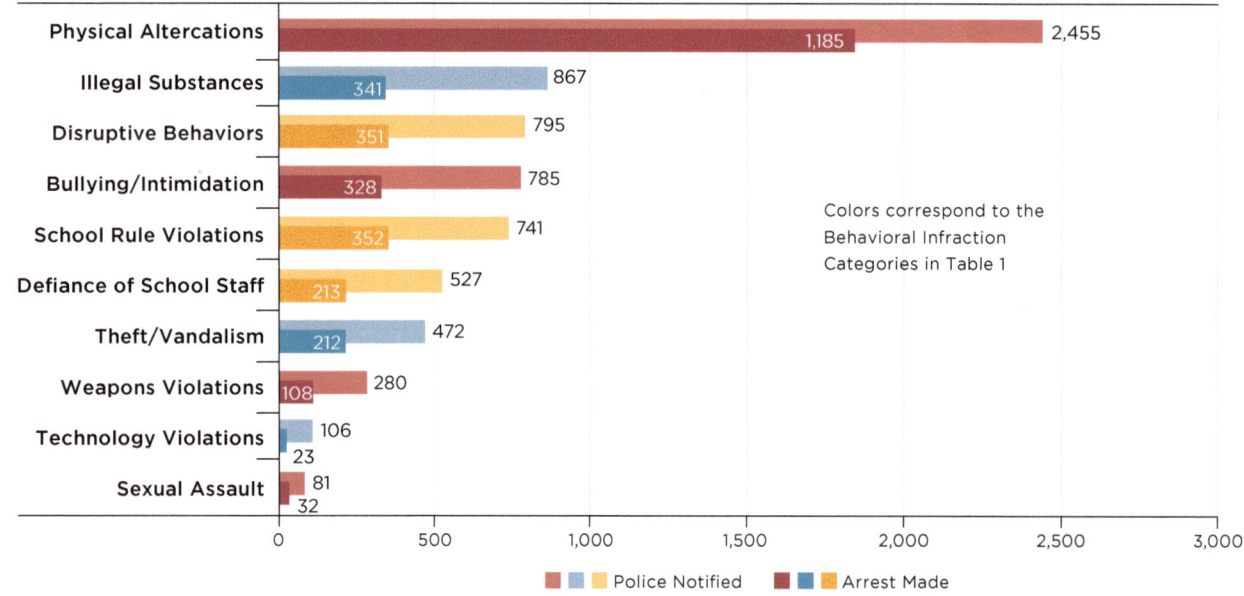

Note: This figure shows the number of police responses to infractions occurring across all high schools, based on *"Type of Infraction."* Categories represent aggregations created for this report and do not reflect official CPS designations. These calculations are based on school administrative data on student misconduct. See Appendix B for which misconduct codes are classified within each category. Police are assumed to have been notified for a given reported infraction whenever a police arrest was made. The number of infractions for which there were arrests is a subset of the number for which police were notified—as indicated by the overlaid arrest bar. The sample of infractions used in these calculations is limited to infractions in CPS groups 3-6 for students in grades 6-12.

FIGURE 17

When Illegal Incidents like Substance Abuse or Theft Occur at School, Police are Most Likely to be Involved

Rates of Police Responses by Type of Infraction (Elementary and High Schools in 2012-13)

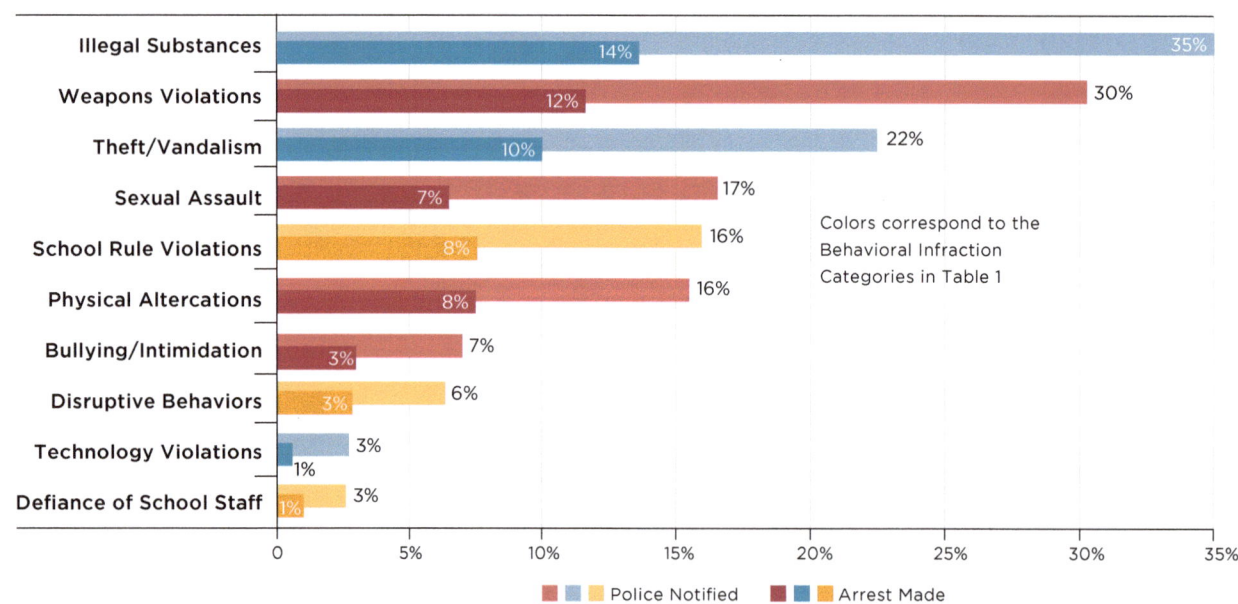

Note: This figure shows the number of police responses to infractions occurring across all high schools, based on *"Type of Infraction."* Categories represent aggregations created for this report and do not reflect official CPS designations. These calculations are based on school administrative data on student misconduct. See Appendix B for which misconduct codes are classified within each category. Police are assumed to have been notified for a given reported infraction whenever a police arrest was made. The number of infractions for which there were arrests is a subset of the number for which police were notified—as indicated by the overlaid arrest bar. The sample of infractions used in these calculations is limited to infractions in CPS groups 3-6 for students in grades 6-12.

CHAPTER 3

Perceptions of School Safety and Order

It is difficult to contextualize the suspension rate trends presented in Chapter 1 without knowing whether the climate of safety and order in schools has changed over time. School administrators are charged with maintaining an orderly school environment; suspensions are one of the primary tools that they use to enforce expected student behavior. Given the emphasis on reducing the use of exclusionary disciplinary practices, one might wonder whether reductions in suspensions have been accompanied by more problems with safety and order. Conversely, the reduced numbers of suspensions could indicate that schools are facing fewer disciplinary problems, so administrators do not feel they need to assign suspensions to students. In fact, this latter statement is consistent with students' and teachers' reports about what is happening in their schools, as described below.

Questions on the My Voice, My School surveys capture students' and teachers' perspectives about their experiences in school. Students reported on how safe they feel at various locations in and around their schools, while teachers were asked to report the extent of various problems at their schools (e.g., student disrespect of teachers, physical conflicts among students, and gang activity). Teachers' and students' responses in 2013-14 are shown in **Figures 18 and 19**, respectively. Because elementary schools in Chicago generally serve students in pre-kindergarten through eighth grade, we are not able to differentiate responses from middle grades teachers from teachers in lower grade levels. Therefore, we only present responses from high school teachers.

High school teachers perceive student disrespect of teachers to be the most common disciplinary problem. About half of teachers report student disrespect of teachers is at least somewhat of a problem (**see Figure 18**). At the same time, teachers also report there are a number of other disciplinary problems in their schools. About 10-15 percent of high school teachers believe there are substantial problems with gang activity, fights among students, and disorder and theft in their buildings, and about half of high school teachers say these issues are somewhat of a problem.

FIGURE 18

Many Teachers Report Problems with Student Disrespect in Their School

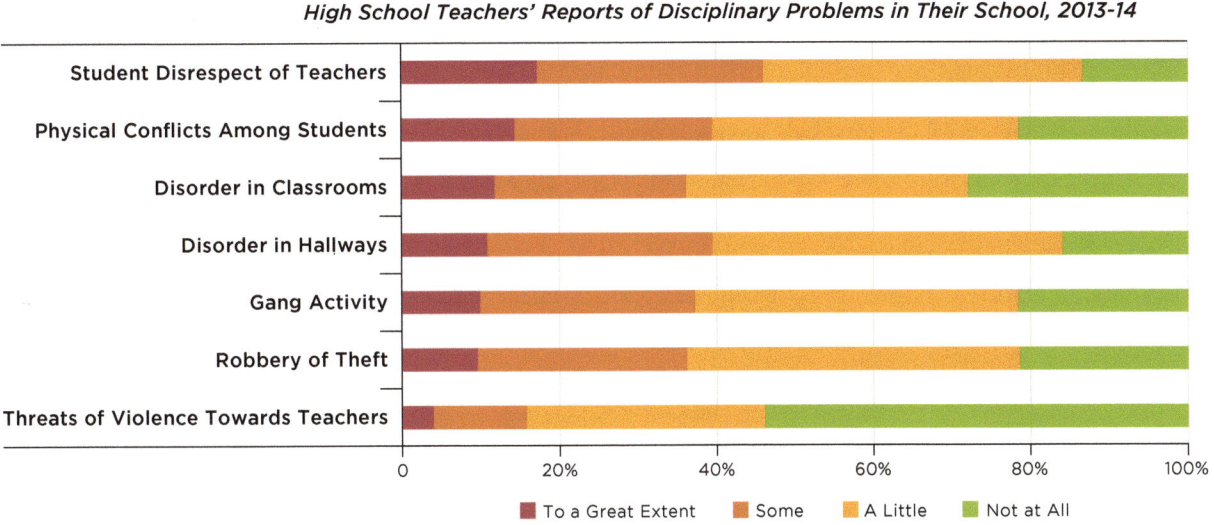

High School Teachers' Reports of Disciplinary Problems in Their School, 2013-14

Note: This figure includes teacher responses to the 2013-14 My Voice, My School Teacher Survey. Charter schools, alternative schools, and special education schools are not included. See Appendix D for details on the survey, including response rates and question wording.

FIGURE 19

Students Feel Safest in Places with a Stronger Adult Presence

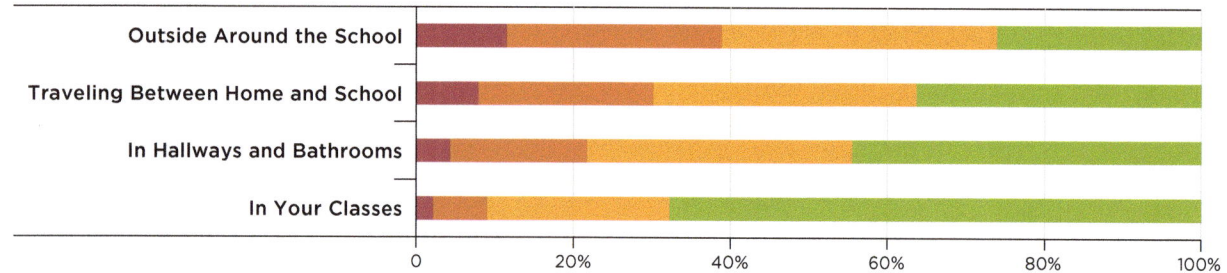

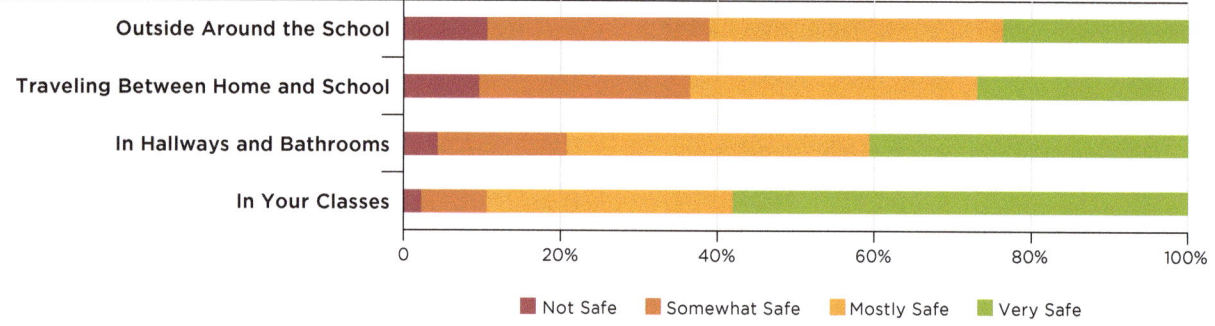

Note: This figure includes responses from sixth- to twelfth-grade students to the 2013-14 My Voice, My School Student Survey. Charter schools, alternative schools, and special education schools are not included. See Appendix D for details on the survey, including response rates and question wording.

Students feel the most safe when they are in environments with strong adult presence. The surveys ask students about how safe they feel in different areas of the school, or on their route to and from school. Almost all students across grade levels—about 90 percent—feel mostly or very safe in their classrooms (**see Figure 19**). However, only about 60 percent of students feel mostly or very safe outside around the school where there is less adult supervision. The area just outside of the school is the place that students feel the least safe—even less safe than when traveling between home and school. This is an area that all students must pass through, but there are often fewer adults to monitor student behavior in this area than there are inside of the school building.

High school students' and teachers' perceptions of safety and order have improved over time. These same questions about school safety and discipline have been asked of students and teachers across school years, so we can track how students' and teachers' perceptions of their schools have changed over time. To track overall changes in climate, the questions are combined into measures that capture students' and teachers' overall perceptions. **Figure 20** shows trends in students' and teachers' reports of safety between 2006-07 and 2013-14.

While about half of high school teachers say they face at least some problems in terms of conflict, disruption, and disorder at their schools, they are reporting climates that are much safer, less disruptive, and more orderly than they were in 2006-07 (**see Figure 20**). High school teachers reported substantially fewer disciplinary problems from the 2008-09 school year to the 2011-12 school year; this is consistent with the period of the Culture of Calm, which targeted a number of high schools. There were no improvements in the 2012-13 school year, but then a sharp improvement was seen again in the 2013-14 school year.

High school students' reports of their perceptions of safety at school generally mirror those of high school teachers; after no improvement from 2006-07 to 2008-09, they reported feeling more safe at school

FIGURE 20

Students' and Teachers' Reports of School Safety and Order Have Been Improving

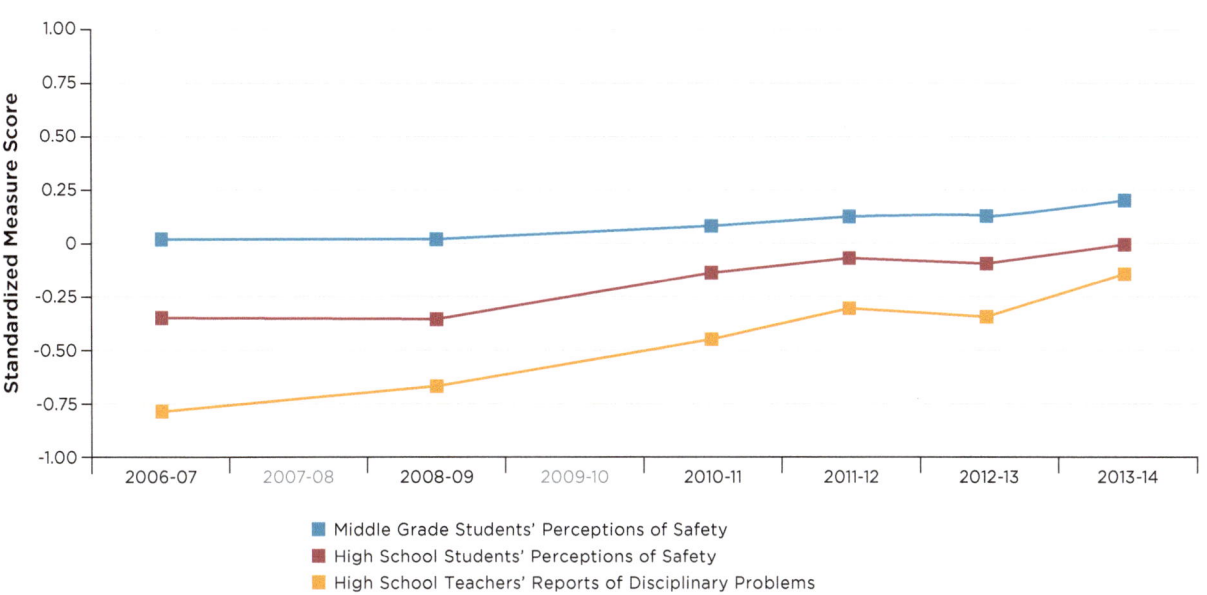

Trends in Reports of Safety and Disciplinary Problems

■ Middle Grade Students' Perceptions of Safety
■ High School Students' Perceptions of Safety
■ High School Teachers' Reports of Disciplinary Problems

Note: The scores on the vertical axis were standardized based on the mean and standard deviation of the measure in 2012-13. A score of zero represents an average level of disciplinary problems or safety in 2012-13 across all CPS schools. Teachers' reports of disciplinary problems were reverse coded so that more positive scores mean fewer problems. Scores that are less than zero indicate that the teacher or student reported feeling less safety and order than was typical in 2012-13, while scores that are greater than zero indicate the teacher or student felt more safe than was typical in 2012-13. A score of -1 is at about the 16th percentile of all schools and years, while a score of +1 is at about the 84th percentile. The teacher and student measures capture different perceptions of the school environment, and cannot be compared to each other. Surveys were administered every other year until 2010-11 when they were administered every year, therefore this figure does not include data for 2007-08 and 2009-10.

from 2008-2009 to 2011-12. There were no improvements in high school students' feelings of safety in 2012-13, and then they improved again in 2013-14.

In the middle grades, students' feelings of safety improved only very slightly from 2006-07 through 2011-12. There was no improvement in the 2012-13 school year, but another slight uptick was seen in the 2013-14 school year.

The improvements in students' and teachers' perceptions of safety roughly correspond to the periods of decline in high school suspension rates. There were no declines in suspension rates before the 2009-10 school year, but there were steady declines in suspension rates in high schools only from 2009-10 through 2011-12; this is the period of improving perceptions of safety among students and teachers in high schools (**see Figure 1 on p.11**). In 2013-14, there was a noticeable decline in suspension rates in both the middle and high school grades, and there were also improvements in students' and teachers' reports of safety in this year, at both the middle grades and high school levels.

School climate has been improving slightly in CPS schools, at the same time that schools have been less likely to use exclusionary disciplinary practices. It could be that schools are seeing less of a need to use exclusionary practices because of improvements in school climate, or that school climate is improving because schools are using disciplinary practices more effectively over time. Regardless of the reason for these trends, at the very least, they suggest that the declining use of suspension rates has not led to a worsening of school climate. At best, they suggest that new practices in Chicago schools may be reducing schools' reliance on exclusionary practices. At the same time, the district still has a great deal of work to do to improve the instructional climate for middle grade and high school students. Many students and teachers still report problems with safety and order at a number of schools in the district, and high school students continue to be at high risk for being suspended.

CHAPTER 4

Interpretive Summary

Chicago Public Schools exemplifies patterns in the use of exclusionary discipline practices across the country. Suspension rates are high, especially for high school students. Schools disproportionately suspend and arrest African American students compared to other student groups. And most students are suspended for behaviors that challenge adult authority and school rules, rather than behaviors that directly threaten the safety of the school environment.

Taking a long-term perspective, district trends give reason for both optimism and pause. On one hand, out-of-school suspension (OSS) and arrest rates have been declining over the last several years. These downward trends started before changes to CPS's Student Code of Conduct (SCC) and may have been facilitated by the earlier Culture of Calm Initiative, at least in high schools. In addition, requirements limiting the number of days for which students can be suspended per incident seem to have had an immediate impact on the length of out-of-school suspensions, especially in high schools. Yet, in-school suspension (ISS) rates for African American high school students are at an all-time high, with big jumps occurring over the last two years. While students receiving an ISS are technically in school, they are still missing classroom instruction. Research suggests that even small amounts of absence can have substantial long-term consequences on educational attainment.[25] Thus, an ISS may still lead students to fall behind in their courses, even if they remain in the building. These trends also suggest that disparities across racial/ethnic groups may continue to grow in the future without significant changes in disciplinary practices, especially for African American students.

These findings raise several issues for the district, schools, and policymakers to consider as they attempt to reduce the use of exclusionary discipline practices.

Since most suspensions are for non-violent, non-threatening incidents, schools might be able to reduce their use without compromising safety. One concern that school administrators have about limiting the use of suspensions is that there may be a trade-off in terms of school safety. Yet, the high percentage of suspensions for non-violent behaviors (e.g., disruption, defiance, and school-rules violation) suggests potential opportunities for reducing student suspensions without compromising the safety of school communities. Some studies suggest using suspensions for things like defiance and disruption reflect the need to support teachers' instructional and de-escalation skills, as well as supporting students' positive behaviors and social-emotional learning.[26] Teachers need to maintain an orderly classroom in order to do their jobs of teaching and promoting student learning and disruptive students can prevent this.[27] This can be frustrating not only because teachers feel personally disrespected but also because they worry about other students in the

---

25 Allensworth & Easton (2007).
26 McFarland (2001); Vavrus & Cole (2002).
27 Classroom order—the degree to which students are doing the work that is expected in their class—is the strongest predictor of learning gains among different elements of classroom instruction. For students to learn, classes need to be both orderly and challenging (Allensworth, Gwynne, Pareja, Sebastian, & Stevens, 2014; Gates Foundation, 2010).

class being able to learn. Providing teachers and school administrators with support and training on behavioral management, and developing effective systems for helping teachers deal with disruptive student behavior, is needed if they are to reduce their reliance on exclusionary practices. This is particularly critical in high schools, where suspensions are most common.

Teachers who have large numbers of students with low achievement levels need support in developing strong skills in classroom management and conflict resolution. Students with low achievement and disabilities are much more likely to get suspended than other students. This can exacerbate their problems in school, as missing class can cause them to fall even further behind. Other UChicago CCSR studies have found that classrooms that serve students with low incoming achievement are much more likely than classrooms with high-achieving students to have problems with student behavior—even when they have similar teachers and similar subjects.[28] Likewise, the school characteristic that is most strongly associated with low levels of safety is the average incoming achievement level of students at the school. In fact, school safety is more strongly related to the incoming academic skills of the student body than to poverty or crime in the neighborhood of the school, or in the neighborhoods where its students live.[29] There is a need to recognize the higher demands on teachers and school staff who provide instruction to students who have struggled with school in the past; they need to have particularly strong skills around engaging and supporting students in learning, as well as in managing potential conflicts that arise.

There is a need to better understand the consequences of replacing out-of-school suspensions with in-school suspensions. The changes that CPS made in 2012 to their SCC seem to have encouraged schools to reduce their use of out-of-school suspensions. However, these changes did not discourage them from using in-school suspensions; instead, these changes may have contributed to their growing use. In the absence of clear alternatives to out-of-school suspensions, staff at some schools may have simply responded to the new directives by issuing in-school suspensions in their place. It could be that in-school suspensions are more effective than out-of-school suspensions, or at least potentially less harmful. Some students might view in-school suspensions as a more salient punishment. Some schools—as recommended by current district initiatives—might use in-school suspensions in a way that keeps students from falling behind in their classes. On the other hand, the differences in their consequences for student engagement in school and the prevention of future problems might not be much different than those for out-of-school suspensions. And there are potential costs to using in-school suspensions in schools, as they require space and staff to enact. If the district is to reduce the overall use of suspensions in high schools, it may need to provide school leaders with concrete, alternative responses to OSS in order to help them avoid turning to other exclusionary practices.

The district still has substantial work to do if it is to reduce disciplinary disparities by student subgroups. Even though suspension and arrest rates have declined over the last five years, Chicago still has very high suspension rates for African American high school students, students with disabilities, and students with weak academic skills. African American high school boys are at particular risk of being suspended or arrested in any given year. This leads to questions about what can be done to reduce the discipline disparities that exist.

One issue is the degree to which students in the same school are at different levels of risk for suspension, based on the structures that are in place at the school around discipline. To address within-school disparities, schools might consider comparing their suspension rates based on students' race, gender, disability status, and incoming achievement levels to discern different levels of suspension risk for their students and to develop strategies to reduce those disparities.

Another issue is the degree to which there are

---

[28] Allensworth, Gwynne, Pareja, Sebastian, & Stevens (2014).
[29] Steinberg et al. (2010).

differences in disciplinary practices across schools serving different populations of students. As will be shown in the next report, there are large differences across schools in suspension rates, and the schools with the largest suspension rates tend to have three characteristics in common: 1) they are high schools, 2) they predominantly serve African American students, and 3) the average incoming achievement levels of their students are below the district average. As long as there are large differences in practices across schools that serve different populations of students, there will be substantial discipline disparities in the district.

Coming Next: Variation in Discipline Practices Across Schools

This report is the first step in understanding discipline practices in CPS. While districtwide trends are helpful, it is at the school level that districtwide policies are translated into outcomes for students. The next report will show how schools vary in their approaches to discipline. It will answer questions such as:

- What is the variation in suspension rates across schools and among schools that serve similar student populations?
- Which types of schools are more likely to suspend students than others?
- How are schools' exclusionary disciplinary practices related to school climate and to the quality of the classroom instructional environment?

A third report in the series will examine the use of alternative and preventative discipline strategies in CPS schools. Subsequent work will examine the consequences of changes in disciplinary policies for changes in school practices around discipline, as well as changes in school climate and instruction.

References

Allensworth, E..M., Gwynne, J.A., Moore, P., & de la Torre, M. (2014).
Looking forward to high school and college: Middle grade indicators of readiness in Chicago Public Schools. Chicago, IL: University of Chicago Consortium on Chicago School Research.

Allensworth, E.M., Gwynne, J.A., Pareja, A.S., Sebastian, J., & Stevens, W.D. (2014).
Free to fail or on-track to college: Setting the stage for academic challenge; classroom control and support. Chicago, IL: University of Chicago Consortium on Chicago School Research.

Allensworth, E.M., & Easton, J.Q. (2007).
What matters for staying on-track and graduating in Chicago Public Schools. Chicago, IL: University of Chicago Consortium on Chicago School Research.

Allensworth, E., Ponisciak, S., & Mazzeo, C. (2009).
The schools teachers leave: Teacher mobility in Chicago Public Schools. Chicago, IL: University of Chicago Consortium on Chicago School Research.

Alvarez, L. (2013, December 3).
Seeing the toll, schools revisit zero tolerance. *New York Times.* Retrieved from http://www.nytimes.com/2013/12/03/education/seeing-the-toll-schools-revisit-zero-tolerance.html?_r=0

American Academy of Pediatrics Committee on School Health. (2003).
Out-of-school suspension and expulsion. *Pediatrics, 112* (5), 1206-1209.

American Psychological Association Zero Tolerance Task Force. (2008).
Are zero tolerance policies effective in schools? An Evidentiary Review and Recommendations. *American Psychologist, 63*(9), 852–862.

Balfanz, R., Byrnes, V., & Fox, J. (2013).
Sent home and put off-track: The antecedents, disproportionalities, and consequences of being suspended in the ninth grade. In D. Losen (Ed.), *Closing the school discipline gap: Research for policymakers.* New York, NY: Teachers College Press.

Balfanz, R., Herzog, L., & MacIver, D.J. (2007).
Preventing student disengagement and keeping students on the graduation path in urban middle grades schools: Early identification and effective interventions. *Educational Psychologist, 42*(4), 223-235.

Bryk, A.S., Sebring, P.B., Allensworth, E., Luppescu, S., & Easton, J.Q. (2010).
Organizing schools for improvement: Lessons from Chicago. Chicago, IL: University of Chicago Press.

Chicago Public Schools Office of Social and Emotional Learning. (n.d.)
Strategies. Retrieved from https://sites.google.com/site/cpspositivebehavior/home/about-positive-behavior-supports/strategies

Chicago Public Schools. (2012).
Student Code of Conduct. Chicago, IL: Chicago Public Schools.

Chicago Public Schools. (2014a).
CPS sees 36 percent drop in suspensions. Retrieved from http://cps.edu/News/Press_releases/Pages/PR1_02_07_2014.aspx

Chicago Public Schools. (2014b).
CPS suspensions and expulsions reduction plan and data highlights. Retrieved from http://www.cpsboe.org/content/documents/student_suspension_and_expulsion_reduction_plan.pdf

Chicago Public Schools. (2014c).
Improving student safety and school climate in Chicago Public Schools. Retrieved from http://www.cityofchicago.org/content/dam/city/depts/mayor/Press%20Room/Press%20Releases/2014/July/07.02.14SafeCpsreport.pdf

Dawson, D.A. (1991).
Family structure and children's health and well-being: Data from the 1988 National Health Interview Survey on Child Health. *Journal of Marriage and Family, 53*(3), 573-584.

Fabelo, T., Thompson, M.D., Plotkin, M., Carmichael, D., Marchbanks, M.P. III, & Booth, E.A. (2011).
Breaking schools' rules: A statewide study of how school discipline relates to students' success and juvenile justice involvement. New York, NY: Council of State Governments Justice Center.

Finn, J.D., & Servos, T.J. (2013).
Misbehavior, suspensions, and security measures in high school: Racial/ethnic and gender differences. In D. Losen (Ed.), *Closing the school discipline gap: Research for policymakers.* New York, NY: Teachers College Press.

Gates Foundation. (2010).
Learning about teaching: Initial findings from the measures of effective teaching project. Retrieved from http://www.metproject.org/downloads/Preliminary_Findings-Research_Paper.pdf

Hatch, A.J. (2002).
Doing qualitative research in education settings. Albany, NY: State University of New York Press.

Heaviside, S., Rowand, C., Williams, C., & Farris, E. (1998).
Violence and discipline problems in U.S. public Schools: 1996-97. (NCES 98030). U.S. Department of Education. Washington, DC: National Center for Education Statistics. Retrieved from http://nces.ed.gov/pubs98/98030.pdf

Himmelstein, K.E.W., & Brückner, H. (2010).
Criminal-justice and school sanctions against nonheterosexual youth: A national longitudinal study. *Pediatrics, 127* (1), 49-57.

Kieffer, M.J., & Marinell, W.H. (2012).
Navigating the middle grades: Evidence from New York City. New York, NY: Research Alliance for New York City Schools.

Kwong, J. (2014, February 26).
SFUSD board approves measure favoring alternatives to suspensions. *The San Francisco Examiner.* Retrieved from http://www.sfexaminer.com/sanfrancisco/sfusd-board-approves-measure-favoring-alternatives-to-suspensions/Content?oid=2715041

LeCompte, M.D., & Preissle, J. (1993).
Ethnography and qualitative design in educational research (2nd Ed.). New York, NY: Academic Press.

Losen, D.J., Hewitt, D., & Toldson, I. (2014).
Eliminating excessive and unfair exclusionary discipline in schools policy recommendations for reducing disparities. Bloomington, IN: The Equity Project at Indiana University.

Losen, D.J., & Gillespie, J. (2012).
Opportunities suspended: The disparate impact of disciplinary exclusion from school. Los Angeles, CA: The Civil Rights Project/Proyecto Derechoes Civiles.

Losen, D.J., & Martinez, T. (2013).
Out of school and off track: The overuse of suspensions in American middle and high schools. Los, Angeles, CA: The Civil Rights Project/Proyecto Derechoes Civiles.

Mattison, E., & Amber, M.S. (2007).
Closing the achievement gap: The association of racial climate with achievement and behavioral outcomes. *American Journal of Community Psychology, 40*(1-2), 1-12.

McFarland, D.A. (2001).
Student resistance: How the formal and informal organization of classrooms facilitate everyday forms of student defiance. *American Journal of Sociology, 107*(3), 612-678.

Neild, R.C., & Balfanz, R. (2006).
Unfulfilled promise: The dimensions and characteristics of Philadelphia's dropout crisis, 2000-05. Philadelphia, PA: Philadelphia Youth Transitions Collaborative.

Osher, D., Bear, G.G., Sprague, J.R., & Doyle, W. (2010).
How can we improve school discipline? *Educational Researcher, 39*(1), 48-58.

Porowski, A., O'Conner, R., & Aikaterini, P. (2014).
Disproportionality in school discipline: An assessment of trends in Maryland, 2009-12. Washington, DC: U.S. Department of Education, Institute of Education Sciences, National Center for Education and Regional Assistance, Regional Educational Laboratory Mid-Atlantic.

Schreck, C.J., & Miller, J.M. (2003).
Sources of fear of crime at school: What is the relative contribution of disorder, individual characteristics, and school security. *Journal of School Violence, 2*(4), 57–79.

Shah, N., & McNeil, M. (2013).
Suspension, expulsion data cast some in harsh light. *Education Week Quality Counts, 32*(16), 12.

Skiba, R.J., Horner, R.H., Chung, C., Rausch, M.K., May, S.L., & Tobin, T. (2011).
Race is not neutral: A national investigation of African American and Latino disproportionality in school discipline. *School Psychology Review, 40*(1), 85-107.

Skiba, R.J., & Rausch, M.K. (2010).
Suspended education: Urban middle schools in crisis. Los Angeles, CA: Civil Rights Project at UCLA.

Skiba, R.J., Shure, L., & Williams, N. (2012).
Racial and ethnic disproportionality in suspension and expulsion. In A.L. Noltemeyer & C.S. Mcloughlin (Eds.), *Disproportionality in education and special education: A guide to creating more equitable learning environments.* Springfield, IL: Charles C. Thomas Publisher, Ltd.

Steinberg, M., Allensworth, E., & Johnson, W.D. (2011).
Student and teacher safety in Chicago Public Schools: The roles of community context and school social organization. Chicago, IL: University of Chicago Consortium on Chicago School Research.

U.S. Department of Education. (2014).
Guiding principals: A resource guide for improving school climate & discipline. Washington, DC: U.S. Department of Education.

Vavrus, F., & Cole, K.M. (2002).
'I didn't do nothing': The discursive construction of school suspension. *The Urban Review, 34*(2), 87-111.

Watanabe, T. (2013, May 14).
L.A. Unified bans suspension for 'willful defiance.' *The Los Angeles Times.* Retrieved from http://articles.latimes.com/print/2013/may/14/local/la-me-lausd-suspension-20130515

Welch, K., & Payne, A.A. (2010).
Racial threat and punitive school discipline. *Social Problems, 57*(1), 25-48.

Appendix A
Data and Methods

Schools and Years Included

This study examines discipline practices during the 2012-13 and 2013-14 school years and the ways in which the use of exclusionary practices and behavioral challenges have changed since 2008-09. It incorporates administrative data from two sources: 1) Chicago Public Schools (CPS) administrative records on suspensions and disciplinary infractions from 2008-09 to 2013-14, and 2) data from the Chicago Police Department (CPD) on arrests from 2006-07 to 2011-12. We also use information from interviews of administrators that were conducted for this study in the spring and early summer of 2013.

For CPS administrative data, we identify students in grades 6-12 (the middle grades and high school years) who are enrolled in regular schools—this does not include students in alternative, special education, or charter schools. Students were considered enrolled if they were enrolled in a CPS school in September and/or May of that school year. All students who are actively enrolled in grades 6-12 are included in the analyses of trends in arrest rates from CPD data, including students attending neighborhood, vocational, charter, and selective schools. (**See Table A.1** for sample size.)

Alternative schools—those designed for re-enrollment of dropouts—and schools for severely disabled students are substantially different from other schools in the district in many ways and they are not comparable to regular CPS schools in terms of discipline or instructional measures. Therefore, they are not included in this study. Charter schools do not provide consistent administrative data on misconduct across all years to CPS, and some schools use their own specific discipline codes, which are not comparable to district records. Therefore, they cannot be included in the analyses of suspensions or infractions. Charter schools are included in the analysis of trends in arrests. The trends for arrest rates look similar, whether or not charter schools are included.

Discipline Records

CPS administrative files contain information on the student infractions that are reported when disciplinary incidents occur. These records tell us why students are getting in trouble, how many students were involved in the incident, and each of the infractions that comprised the incident.

While these administrative files tell us which students are getting in trouble, and for what types of infractions, they may not necessarily provide a complete assessment of the problems that are occurring at schools. Schools may not be consistent in the degree to

TABLE A.1

Sample Size by Grade and Year

School Year	Analysis Using CPS Data		Analysis Using CPD Data	
	Middle Grade Students (N)	High School Students (N)	Middle Grade Students (N)	High School Students (N)
2006-07	—	—	88,502	108,546
2007-08	—	—	87,075	108,546
2008-09	86,274	100,970	89,555	110,993
2009-10	82,254	99,654	86,288	112,739
2010-11	79,574	95,384	84,540	111,513
2011-12	78,606	92,926	84,484	111,179
2012-13	77,337	90,049	—	—
2013-14	74,955	87,364	—	—

which they are aware of incidents or how they report incidents, or the way that they record incidents if a student does not receive a suspension. In our interviews with administrators, we learned that in some high schools, lower-level infractions often were not reported at all, particularly if they did not result in a suspension. This is consistent with the data in the discipline files; low-level infractions (falling in Groups 1 or 2) are much more rarely seen in the data than incidents that would be expected to occur at much lower rates (falling in Group 3 or higher). Almost all of the infractions that are reported (87 percent) include a suspension, which also suggests that schools rarely report infractions unless they result in a suspension.

Disciplinary incidents can include multiple infractions and multiple students. One particular student may have multiple infractions associated with an incident. For example, if an incident involves both bullying and a physical fight between two students, one student may receive an infraction of *"Fighting: Two people, no injuries,"* and the other may receive that infraction as well as *"Intimidation/Threats/Coercion/Severe Bullying."* In our analysis, in order to avoid inflating the number of instances of misconduct, we focus on counts of incidents rather than infractions. In cases where infractions of two different types are reported for the same incident for the same student, we use the most serious infraction to define the incident for the student.

Police Records

CPD data provide information on all arrests and reported criminal incidents in Chicago. These records identify individuals arrested, the location and date of the arrest, the location and date of the incident, and a description of the charges.

Chapin Hall matched the CPD data to CPS administrative data to identify arrest records for all students in this study. Student names in the CPS administrative records (for all students enrolled in 1991 through fall 2013) and the CPD data (all arrests occurring from 2000 through 2012) were cleaned and standardized. Each component of the name (last, first, and middle) was scanned in order to remove unwanted characters and to correct embedded names (i.e., two names in one name field). MatchWorks' AutoStan program was used for name standardization. De-duplication and matching were done using AutoMatch software. Fields included in the match were first name, middle name or initial, last name, birth date, race, and gender. Matches are performed separately from analysis on suspensions and arrests, and names are removed before analysis; analysts, therefore, have an ID number but do not know the identity of subjects.

Arrest records were obtained for all students who were actively enrolled in grades 6-12 during the years being studied. Students who left CPS are included in the analyses for the years in which they were actively enrolled. These include arrests at school and outside of school. At the time of this report, CPD data were only available through December 2012, so we are only able to report on arrests using this data set through school year 2011-12.

Qualitative Interviews

To better understand why schools use different disciplinary approaches, one administrator at each of 20 schools was interviewed in the late spring and summer of 2013. The semi-structured interviews, which were done on location at the interviewee's school, varied in length and number of sessions but took on average 1.75 hours across one to three sessions. The schools consisted of 10 high schools and 10 schools serving middle grades that were selected to participate based on different school and student populations, as described below.

School sample selection for the qualitative interviews.
We used CPS administrative data to guide the selection process for the schools in which we interviewed administrators. We compared actual suspension rates to rates of suspensions that were predicted by prior student achievement, as well as the prevalence of crime and poverty in the students' home neighborhoods. This comparison was used to identify three strata of schools: 1) schools suspending more than other schools serving similar student populations, 2) schools with similar suspension rates to other schools serving similar student populations, and 3) schools with lower suspension rates than other schools serving similar student populations. We then stratified explicitly on race—

identifying schools that were majority African American (more than 65 percent of students) and those that were not. We stratified by race because, on average, suspension rates were substantially higher in schools that predominantly served African American students; without this stratification, the three categories would have largely been defined based on their racial composition. Once schools were categorized, we randomly selected high schools and schools serving the middle grades from within each of the categories shown in **Table A.2**.

Interviews were conducted with staff who were considered the best contact person from their school to speak about discipline practices and policies in their school, which included principals, assistant principals, deans, and/or dean supervisors. We reached out to schools by calling the school main office number and relied on them to direct us to the appropriate person (*"the individual in charge of discipline in your school"*). In situations where they were uncertain, we asked for a school contact who could better direct us.

Our qualitative data was analyzed using typological analysis. Interviews were transcribed and entered into the ATLAS.ti qualitative software program. Transcript quotes were then labeled according to broad themes that paralleled the interview protocol. This process facilitated data management, allowing us to easily sort and retrieve data for further analysis. Working with general themes individually, we coded transcripts excerpts inductively for emerging patterns.

TABLE A.2
Sampling Scheme for Interview Schools

Comparison of Actual to Predicted Suspension Rates	Majority African American	Majority Not African American
Higher Suspension Rate than Expected	2 Middle Grade Schools 2 High Schools	2 Middle Grade Schools 2 High Schools
Suspension Rate about as Expected	1 Middle Grade School 1 High School	1 Middle Grade School 1 High School
Lower Suspension Rate than Expected	2 Middle Grade Schools 2 High Schools	2 Middle Grade Schools 2 High Schools

---

30 Hatch (2002); LeCompte & Preissle (1993).

Appendix B
Infractions and Codes

In Chapter 2, we discuss behavior categories and behavior groups that we developed using the 2012-13 Chicago Public Schools Student Code of Conduct (SCC). In **Table B.1**, numbers in the left-hand column correspond with infraction codes in the SCC. The first number is the infraction group. The SCC categorizes infractions into six different groups, according to the extent to which the infraction disrupts the learning environment. The second number denotes the nature of the infraction. For more information on infraction codes, see the SCC: http://cps.edu/Pages/StudentCodeofConduct.aspx. We split the 216 SCC infractions into three main categories shown in these appendix tables. Note that these are not CPS-defined categories.

TABLE B.1
Defiance and School Rules Violations

Defiance of School Staff	
2-8	Defying (disobeying) the authority of school personnel.
3-5	Persisting in serious acts of disobedience or inappropriate behaviors listed in Groups 1 through 3 of this SCC.
5-5	Persistent defiance of multiple directives by school personnel resulting in the most serious disruption of the educational process.
Disruptive Behaviors	
1-1	Running and/or making excessive noise in the hall or building.
1-2	Leaving the classroom without permission.
1-3	Engaging in any behavior that is disruptive to the orderly process of classroom instruction.
2-3	Interfering with school authorities and programs through walkouts or sit-ins.
2-4	Initiating or participating in any unacceptable minor physical actions.
2-6	Exhibiting or publishing any profane, obscene, indecent, immoral, libelous, or offensive materials, or using such language or gestures.
3-1	Disruptive behavior on the school bus.
3-6	Any behavior not otherwise listed in Groups 1 through 3 of this SCC that seriously disrupts the educational process.
4-9	Any behavior not otherwise listed in Groups 1 through 4 of this SCC that very seriously disrupts the educational process.
4-10	Disorderly conduct.
5-19	Participating in a mob action—a large or disorderly group of students using force to cause injury to a person or property, or persisting in severe disruption after being directed to cease by school personnel or police.
6-4	Bomb threat—false indication that a bomb, or other explosive of any nature, is concealed in a place that would endanger human life if activated.

TABLE B.1: *CONTINUED*

Defiance and School Rules Violations

Miscellaneous School Rule Violations	
1-4	Loitering, or occupying an unauthorized place in the school or on school grounds.
2-1	Posting or distributing unauthorized written materials on school grounds.
2-5	Failing to abide by school rules and regulations not otherwise listed in the SCC.
2-9	Failing to provide proper identification.
2-10	Unauthorized use of school parking lots or other areas.
3-2	Gambling—participating in games of chance or skill for money or things of value.
3-7	Forgery—false and fraudulent making or altering of a document or the use of such a document.
3-8	Plagiarizing, cheating, and/or copying the work of another student or other source.
3-9	Overt display of gang affiliation.
3-12	Inappropriately wearing any JROTC or Military Academy Uniform on or off school grounds.
4-1	False activation of a fire alarm that does not cause a school facility to be evacuated or does not cause emergency services to be notified.
4-8	Possession, use, sale, or distribution of fireworks.
Miscellaneous School Violations	
4-11	Trespassing on CPS property—entering CPS property when previously prohibited, or remaining on school grounds after receiving a request to depart.
5-6	Gang activity or overt displays of gang affiliation.
5-8	Engaging in any other illegal behavior which interferes with the school's educational process, including attempting an illegal behavior.
5-10	False activation of a fire alarm which causes a school facility to be evacuated or causes emergency services to be notified.
5-16	Inappropriate consensual sexual activity.
Attendance/Truancy	
1-5	Failing to attend class without a valid excuse.
1-6	Persistent tardiness to school or class.
2-2	Leaving the school without permission.

TABLE B.2

Conflicts and Threats to Safety

Physical Altercations	
3-3	Fighting—physical contact between two people with intent to harm, but no injuries result.
4-3	Assault—an attempt or reasonable threat to inflict injury on someone with a show of force that would cause the victim to expect an immediate battery.
4-5	Battery (unwanted bodily contact with another person without legal justification), or aiding or abetting in the commission of a battery which does not result in a physical injury.
4-6	Fighting—physical contact between more than two people with intent to harm, or physical contact between two people with intent to harm that results in injury.
5-1	Aggravated assault—assault with a deadly weapon or done by a person who conceals his/her identity, or any assault against school personnel.
5-12	Battery, or aiding or abetting in the commission of a battery, which results in a physical injury. Battery means unwanted bodily contact with another person without legal justification.
5-13	Initiating or participating in any inappropriate, minor physical contact with school personnel, such as pushing school personnel out of the way in order to physically fight with another student.
6-8	Aggravated battery (battery that causes great harm, is done with a deadly weapon, is done by a person who conceals his/her identity, or the use of physical force against school personnel) or aiding and abetting in the commission of an aggravated battery.
6-10	Attempted murder—an act that constitutes a substantial step toward intended commission of murder.
Sexual Assault	
5-7	Inappropriate sexual conduct, including unwelcomed sexual contact, indecent exposure, transmitting sexually suggestive images through information technology devices, or other sexual activities which do not involve the use of force.
5-9	Persistent or severe acts of sexual harassment—unwelcome sexual or gender-based conduct (either physical or verbal) and/or conduct of a sexual nature which is sufficiently severe, persistent, or pervasive to limit a student's ability to participate in or benefit from the educational program or which creates a hostile or abusive school environment.
6-7	Sex acts which include the use of force.
Weapons Violations	
4-13	Possession of any dangerous object as defined by this SCC: First offense.
5-11	Second or repeated violation of Behavior 4-13; possession of any dangerous object as defined by this SCC.
6-1	Use, possession, and/or concealment of a firearm/destructive device or other weapon or "look-alikes" of weapons as defined in the Additional Resources section, or use or intent to use any other object to inflict bodily harm.
Bullying/Intimidation	
3-4	Profane, obscene, indecent, and immoral or seriously offensive language and gestures, propositions, behavior, or harassment based on race, color, national origin, sex, gender, sexual orientation, age, religion, gender identity, gender expression, or disability.
3-10	Bullying behaviors.
4-2	Extortion—obtaining money or information from another by coercion or intimidation.
5-4	Use of intimidation, credible threats of violence, coercion, or persistent severe bullying. Intimidation is behavior that prevents or discourages another student from exercising his/her right to education, or using force against students, school personnel, and school visitors.
6-5	Robbery—taking personal property in the possession of another by use of force or by threatening the imminent use of force.

TABLE B.3
Illegal Behaviors

	Illegal Substances
2-7	Possession (physical control over items, such as contained in clothing, lockers, or bags) and/or use of tobacco products, matches, cigarette lighters, or rolling papers.
4-14	Use or possession of alcohol in school or at, before, or after a school related function: first offense.
5-17	Use or possession of illegal drugs, narcotics, controlled substances, "look-alikes" of such substances, or contraband, or use of any other substance for the purpose of intoxication in or before school or a school-related function.
5-18	Second or repeated violation of Behavior 4-14, use or possession of alcohol in school or at, before, or after a school-related function.
6-6	Sale, distribution, or intent to sell or distribute alcohol, illegal drugs, narcotics, controlled substances, "look-alikes" of such substances, contraband, or any other substance used for the purpose of intoxication, or repeated violation of Behavior 5-17.
	Technology Violations
1-7	Use of the CPS network for the purpose of accessing noneducational materials, such as games, pornographic materials, and other inappropriate materials.
2-11	Use of the CPS network for the purposes of distributing or downloading noneducational material.
2-12	Possession of cellular telephones or other information technology devices without prior permission of the principal.
3-11	Unauthorized activation or use of cellular telephones or other information technology device.
3-13	Use of the CPS network or any information technology device for any unauthorized purpose not otherwise listed in this SCC.
4-12	Knowingly or intentionally using the CPS network or information technology devices to spread viruses to the CPS network.
5-14	Use of any computer, including social networking websites, or use of any information technology device to threaten, stalk, harass, bully, or otherwise intimidate others, or hacking (intentionally gaining access by illegal means or without authorization) into the CPS network to access student records or other unauthorized information, or to otherwise circumvent the information security system, regardless of intent.
6-2	Intentionally causing or attempting to cause all or a portion of the CPS network to become inoperable.
	Theft/Vandalism
4-4	Vandalism (willful or malicious destruction or defacing of the property of others) or criminal damage to property at a cost less than $500.
4-7	Theft (unauthorized control over the physical property of another) or possession (physical control over, such as contained in clothing, lockers or bags) of stolen property that costs less than $150.
5-2	Theft (obtaining or exerting unauthorized control over) or possession (physical control over, including in clothing, lockers, or bags) of stolen property that costs more than $150.
5-3	Vandalism (willful or malicious destruction or defacing of property) or criminal damage to property that results in damage exceeding $500 or that is done to personal property belonging to any school personnel.
5-15	Burglary knowingly and without authority entering or remaining in a building or vehicle with intent to commit a felony or theft therein.
6-3	Arson—knowingly damaging, by means of fire or explosive, a building and/or the personal property of others.
6-12	Theft (obtaining or exerting unauthorized control over) or possession (physical control over, including in clothing, lockers, or bags) of stolen property that costs more than $1,000.

Appendix C
Police Notification Guidelines

TABLE C.1

Infractions for which Police May Be Contacted or Must Be Contacted, per the 2012-13 Student Code of Conduct

May Contact Police		Must Contact Police	
School Rule Violation		**School Rule Violation**	
4-1	False activation of a fire alarm that does not cause a school facility to be evacuated or does not cause emergency services to be notified.	5-6	Gang activity or overt displays of gang affiliation.
4-8	Possession, use, sale, or distribution of fireworks.	5-10	False activation of a fire alarm which causes a school facility to be evacuated or causes emergency services to be notified.
4-11	Trespassing on CPS property.		
Physical Altercations		**Physical Altercations**	
4-3	Assault	5-1	Aggravated assault.
4-5	Battery, or aiding or abetting in the commission of a battery, which does not result in physical injury.	5-12	Battery, or aiding or abetting in the commission of a battery, which results in a physical injury.
4-6	Fighting—more than two people and/or injuries involved.	5-19	Participating in a mob action.
5-4	Use of intimidation, credible threats of violence, coercion, or persistent severe assault.	6-1	Use, possession, and/or concealment of a firearm/destructive device or other weapon or "look-alikes" of weapons, or use or intent to use any other object to inflict bodily harm.
5-13	Initiating or participating in any inappropriate, minor physical contact with school personnel.	6-8	Aggravated battery, or aiding and abetting in the commission of an aggravated battery.
		6-9	Murder
		6-10	Attempted murder
		6-11	Kidnapping
Sexual Misconduct		**Sexual Misconduct**	
5-7	Inappropriate sexual conduct.	5-9	Persistent or severe acts of sexual harassment.
		6-7	Sex acts which include the use of force.
Substance Abuse and Possession		**Substance Abuse and Possession**	
5-18	Second or repeated violation of code 4-14, use of alcohol in school or at a school related function or before school or before a school-related function.	5-17	Use or possession of illegal drugs, narcotics, controlled substances, "look-alikes" of such substances, or contraband, or use of any substance for the purpose of intoxication in school or at a school-related function or before school or a school-related function.
		6-6	Sale, distribution, or intent to sell or distribute alcohol, illegal drugs, narcotics, controlled substances, or "look-alikes" of such substances, contraband, or any other substance used for the purpose of intoxication; or second or repeated violation of code.
Technology-Related Violation		**Technology-Related Violation**	
		4-12	Knowingly or intentionally using the CPS network or information technology devices to spread viruses to the CPS network.
		5-14	Use of any computer, including social network websites, or use of any information technology device to threaten, stalk, harass, bully, or otherwise intimidate others, or hacking into the CPS network to access student records or other unauthorized information, and/or to otherwise circumvent the information security system.
		6-2	Intentionally causing or attempting to cause all or a portion of the CPS network to become inoperable.

Appendix D
Data from Surveys of Students and Teachers

UChicago CCSR has been partnering with CPS to survey all students in grades 6-12 and all teachers across the district since the early 1990s. This survey, entitled My Voice, My School, was administered in 2007, 2009, and annually from 2011 through 2014. Sets of questions were combined into measures of general concepts, such as students' feelings of safety and teachers' perceptions of crime and disorder, using Rasch analysis.

Students' Perceptions of Safety: Students responded to questions about general feelings of safety asking how safe they feel on their way to and from school, outside around the school, in the hallways and bathrooms of the school, and in their classes. A high score means that students feel very safe.

Teachers' Perceptions of Safety, Crime, and Disorder: Teachers were asked about their perceptions of crime and disorder in the school, including the presence of gang activity, threats of violence toward teachers, disorder in hallways, and disorder in classrooms. We reversed the scores of this measure so that a high score on this measure means that teachers perceive the school to be *more* safe.

Sometimes survey information is seen as subjective. However, there is considerable evidence that these measures are valid instruments of school climate. One source of evidence comes from the strong correlation between students' and teachers' reports of safety and disorder in their schools, even though they come from different sources of information.[31] The relationship of teacher reports of safety with student reports of safety is stronger than the relationship of either with characteristics of the students or neighborhoods they serve, such as crime and poverty. Students' and teachers' reports of safety are also highly predictive of other student and school outcomes. For example, students' reports of school safety are very strongly predictive of how many teachers leave the school before the next school year.[32] They are also predictive of which schools are likely to have stagnant test score and attendance growth.[33]

TABLE D.1

Response Rates across Years for Non-Charter Schools with Students in Grades 6-12.

Year	Grade Level	Number of Responding Students	Students' Response Rate	Number of Responding Teachers	Teachers' Response Rate
2006-07	Elementary	74,202	84%	12,486	76%
	High	60,301	63%	4,283	64%
2008-09	Elementary	65,816	79%	9,020	54%
	High	53,318	58%	3,712	53%
2010-11	Elementary	66,646	86%	7,133	50%
	High	64,113	72%	3,247	53%
2011-12	Elementary	61,578	81%	8,855	64%
	High	61,796	71%	4,258	67%
2012-13	Elementary	64,631	86%	11,608	83%
	High	61,493	73%	4,493	78%
2013-14	Elementary	64,940	91%	11,175	82%
	High	58,080	72%	4,276	79%

Note: At least a 10 percent response rate was required to be considered participating.

---

31 Steinberg et al. (2011).
33 Allensworth, Ponisciak, & Mazzeo (2009).
34 Bryk, Sebring, Allensworth, Luppescu, & Easton (2010).

TABLE D.2

Survey Question Wording for Student and Teacher Reports of Safety and Order

Survey measure	Survey questions
Students' Perceptions of Safety	How safe do you feel:
	1. Outside around the school?
	2. Traveling between home and school?
	3. In the hallways and bathrooms of the school?
	4. In your classes?
	Not Safe, Somewhat Safe, Mostly Safe, Very Safe
Teachers' Perceptions of Safety	To what extent is each of the following a problem at your school:
	1. Physical conflicts among students
	2. Robbery or theft
	3. Gang activity
	4. Disorder in classrooms
	5. Disorder in hallways
	6. Student disrespect of teachers
	7. Threats of violence toward teachers
	Not at All, A Little, Some, To a Great Extent

ABOUT THE AUTHORS

W. DAVID STEVENS is a Manager in the Center for Research, Evaluation, and Assessment at Education Northwest. Stevens has extensive experience leading mixed-methods research projects across a broad range of subject areas including high school reform, teacher human capital, school discipline, school transitions, and district evaluation systems. Prior to joining Education Northwest, Stevens spent 10 years at UChicago CCSR where he was Director of Research Engagement. He received his PhD in sociology from Northwestern University.

LAUREN SARTAIN is a Research Analyst at UChicago CCSR. She has a bachelor's degree from the University of Texas at Austin, as well as a master's degree in Public Policy at the Harris School at the University of Chicago where she is currently a PhD student. She has worked at Chapin Hall and the Federal Reserve Bank of Chicago. Sartain's research interests include principal and teacher quality, school choice, and urban school reform.

ELAINE M. ALLENSWORTH is the Lewis-Sebring Director at UChicago CCSR where she has conducted research on educational policy for the last 15 years. She is best known for her studies of high school graduation and college readiness, and also conducts research in the areas of school leadership and school organization. Her work on early indicators of high school graduation has been adopted for tracking systems used in Chicago and other districts across the country. She is one of the authors of the book *Organizing Schools for Improvement: Lessons from Chicago*, which provides a detailed analysis of school practices and community conditions that promote school improvement. Allensworth holds a PhD in Sociology and an MA in Urban Studies from Michigan State University. She was once a high school Spanish and science teacher.

RACHEL LEVENSTEIN is the Senior Manager for Survey Research at UChicago CCSR, where she oversees the annual census of roughly 225,000 Chicago Public Schools students, teachers, and principals. She directs all aspects of the survey process, including content design and pre-testing, data collection, documentation, item analysis, and tests for response bias. She is also involved in reporting and dissemination of the results to the nearly 700 schools in CPS. Her research specialties include nonresponse and measurement error issues in survey data collection. Rachel received her PhD in survey methodology from the University of Michigan.

This report reflects the interpretation of the authors. Although UChicago CCSR's Steering Committee provided technical advice, no formal endorsement by these individuals, organizations, or the full Consortium should be assumed.

UCHICAGOCCSR

CONSORTIUM ON CHICAGO SCHOOL RESEARCH

Directors

ELAINE M. ALLENSWORTH
Lewis-Sebring Director

EMILY KRONE
Director for Outreach and Communication

JENNY NAGAOKA
Deputy Director

MELISSA RODERICK
*Senior Director
Hermon Dunlap Smith Professor
School of Social Service Administration*

PENNY BENDER SEBRING
Co-Founder

SUE SPORTE
Director for Research Operations

MARISA DE LA TORRE
Director for Internal Research Capacity

Steering Committee

KATHLEEN ST. LOUIS CALIENTO
Co-Chair
Spark, Chicago

KIM ZALENT
Co-Chair
Business and Professional People for the Public Interest

Ex-Officio Members

TIMOTHY KNOWLES
Urban Education Institute

Institutional Members

JOHN R. BARKER
Chicago Public Schools

CLARICE BERRY
Chicago Principals and Administrators Association

AARTI DHUPELIA
Chicago Public Schools

CHRISTOPHER KOCH
Illinois State Board of Education

KAREN G.J. LEWIS
Chicago Teachers Union

SHERRY J. ULERY
Chicago Public Schools

Individual Members

VERONICA ANDERSON
Communications Consultant

JOANNA BROWN
Logan Square Neighborhood Association

CATHERINE DEUTSCH
Illinois Network of Charter Schools

RAQUEL FARMER-HINTON
University of Wisconsin, Milwaukee

KIRABO JACKSON
Northwestern University

CHRIS JONES
Stephen T. Mather High School

DENNIS LACEWELL
Urban Prep Charter Academy for Young Men

LILA LEFF
Umoja Student Development Corporation

RUANDA GARTH MCCULLOUGH
Young Women's Leadership Academy

LUISIANA MELÉNDEZ
Erikson Institute

CRISTINA PACIONE-ZAYAS
Latino Policy Forum

PAIGE PONDER
One Million Degrees

LUIS R. SORIA
Chicago Public Schools

BRIAN SPITTLE
DePaul University

MATTHEW STAGNER
Mathematica Policy Research

AMY TREADWELL
Chicago New Teacher Center

ERIN UNANDER
Al Raby High School

ARIE J. VAN DER PLOEG
American Institutes for Research (Retired)

www.ingramcontent.com/pod-product-compliance
Lightning Source LLC
Chambersburg PA
CBHW060821090426
42738CB00002B/67